Contents

Getting the most from this book

Questions & Answers

Exam-style questions

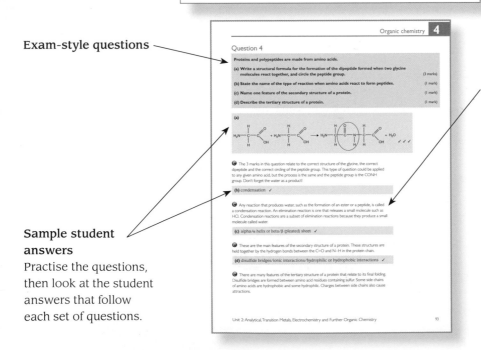

Examiner commentary on sample student answers

Find out how many marks each answer would be awarded in the exam and then read the examiner comments (preceded by the icon **e**) following each student answer.

Sample student answers

Practise the questions, then look at the student answers that follow each set of questions.

About this book

This book will guide you through CCEA A2 Chemistry Unit 2: Analytical, Transition Metals, Electrochemistry and Further Organic Chemistry. It has two sections:

- The **Content Guidance** section covers all of A2 Unit 2 and includes helpful *examiner tips* on how to approach revision and improve exam technique. Do not skim over these tips as they provide important guidance. There are also *knowledge check* questions throughout this section, with *answers* at the end of the book. At the end of each section there is a *summary* of the key points covered.
- The **Questions and Answers** section gives sample examination questions on each topic as well as worked answers and examiner comments on the common pitfalls to avoid. The examination will consist of 10 multiple-choice questions (each with four options, A to D), followed by several structured questions. This Questions and Answers section contains many different examples of questions, but you should also refer to past papers for this unit, which are available online.

Both the Content Guidance and Questions and Answers sections are divided into the topics outlined by the CCEA specification.

General tips

- Be accurate with your learning at this level as examiners will penalise incorrect wording.
- For any calculation, always follow it through to the end even if you feel you have made a mistake, as there are marks for the correct method even if the final answer is incorrect.
- Always attempt to answer a multiple-choice question even if it is a guess (you have a 25% chance of getting it right).

The uniform mark you receive for A2 Unit 2 will be out of 120. Both AS Unit 1 and AS Unit 2 are awarded out of 105 and the AS Unit 3 (examining practical work and planning from AS Unit 1 and AS Unit 2) is awarded out of 90 uniform marks, giving a possible total of 300 for AS chemistry. Both A2 Unit 1 and A2 Unit 2 are awarded out of 120 and the A2 Unit 3 (examining practical work and planning from A2 Unit 1 and A2 Unit 2) is awarded out of 60 uniform marks, giving a possible total of 300 for A2 chemistry. This gives a total of 600 for GCE chemistry. A2 exams will have synoptic questions in which you will have to use your knowledge of AS chemistry.

When answering questions involving the colour of a chemical, you must be accurate to obtain the marks. If the colour of a chemical is given in this book with a hyphen (-) between the colours then state the two colours exactly like that, including the hyphen. For example, chromium(III) hydroxide is a green-blue solid, so both green and blue are required separated by a hyphen.

If two or more colours are given separated by a forward slash (/), these are alternative answers and only *one* colour from this list should be given. For example, for the yellow/orange colour of a solution of Fe^{3+} ions, only yellow on its own or orange on its own will be accepted, but *not* a combination of the two colours.

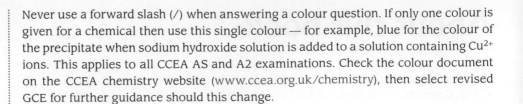

Never use a forward slash (/) when answering a colour question. If only one colour is given for a chemical then use this single colour — for example, blue for the colour of the precipitate when sodium hydroxide solution is added to a solution containing Cu^{2+} ions. This applies to all CCEA AS and A2 examinations. Check the colour document on the CCEA chemistry website (www.ccea.org.uk/chemistry), then select revised GCE for further guidance should this change.

Mass spectrometry

Mass spectrometry is an analytical technique in which a sample can be analysed or identified from its mass spectrum.

The process of mass spectrometry

Mass spectrometry is a process in which a sample is:
1 **vaporised/atomised** — turned into gaseous particles
2 **ionised** — bombarded by electrons to knock off electrons and create singly charged positive ions
3 **accelerated** — made to move rapidly
4 **deflected** — made to follow a path by a magnetic field
5 **detected** — counted as the ions hit an ion detector

The magnetic field in stage 4 above is varied. As all ions have a single positive charge, the mass of the ion determines how deflected it is. Only ions with a mass suitable for the current magnetic field will reach the detector. By varying the magnetic field, all ions and their abundances can be detected.

Uses of mass spectrometry

Mass spectrometry is a technique used to determine the following:
- relative atomic mass (RAM) of elements
- existence of isotopes of elements and their relative abundance
- relative molecular mass (RMM) of compounds (mostly organic)
- presence of halogen atoms
- structure of ions responsible for **fragments** present in the spectrum
- identity of the structure of compounds by comparison of the spectrum with a database of known compounds
- the mechanism of a reaction by labelling an atom (using a heavier isotope such as ^{18}O) and following its path through the reaction

Features of a mass spectrum

- The vertical axis of a mass spectrum is relative abundance; the abundance of all ions is measured relative to the abundance of the **base peak** (usually set to 100).
- The horizontal axis is m/e or m/z (mass to charge ratio); as charges are all +1 then the m/e (m/z) axis is really a mass axis.
- The base peak is the highest/tallest (most abundant) peak in the spectrum (and so it is the peak for the most stable ion).
- The molecular ion peak (M^+) is the last major peak in the spectrum with the highest m/e value.

Examiner tip
The actual process of mass spectrometry is not examined but it is important to understand the process to understand how the ions are produced.

Examiner tip
You should revise the mass spectrometry section of 'Atomic structure' in AS Unit 1 as an introduction before you look at this section because there are synoptic questions at A2 and mass spectrometry could easily be one of them.

A **fragment** ion is a positively charged ion formed when the molecular ion breaks apart.

Examiner tip
The horizontal axis of a mass spectrum should be labelled m/e (or m/z).

- The fragmentation pattern is the pattern of peaks with m/e values lower than the molecular ion peak.
- The $(M+1)^+$ peak is a small peak one m/e value above the M^+ peak. It is caused by the presence of one ^{13}C atom in a molecular ion.
- A major peak at $(M+2)^+$ is caused by the presence of either a Cl or Br atom in the molecule. Both chlorine and bromine have isotopes that differ by two mass units: ^{35}Cl and ^{37}Cl; ^{79}Br and ^{81}Br. The ratio of ^{35}Cl to ^{37}Cl is 3:1, so if the M^+ peak is three times more abundant than the $(M+2)^+$ peak, a Cl atom is present. The ratio of ^{79}Br to ^{81}Br is 1:1 so if the M^+ peak has the same abundance as the $(M+2)^+$ peak, a Br atom is present.

Element mass spectrometry

All isotopes of the elements are shown with their relative abundances. Relative atomic mass (RAM) of the element can be calculated by:
- multiplying the m/e value by the relative abundance for every isotope
- adding all these values together
- dividing by the total of all the relative abundances

The species responsible for peaks are indicated with mass number and charge — for example, $^{65}Zn^+$ or $^{37}Cl^+$. For polyatomic elements such as the halogens, peaks will be seen for the molecules. For example, for chlorine peaks will be seen at:
- 74 caused by $(^{37}Cl-^{37}Cl)^+$
- 72 caused by $(^{35}Cl-^{37}Cl)^+$
- 70 caused by $(^{35}Cl-^{35}Cl)^+$
- 37 caused by $^{37}Cl^+$
- 35 caused by $^{35}Cl^+$

Example of mass spectrum

Figure 1 shows the mass spectrum for ethyl ethanoate, $CH_3COOCH_2CH_3$.

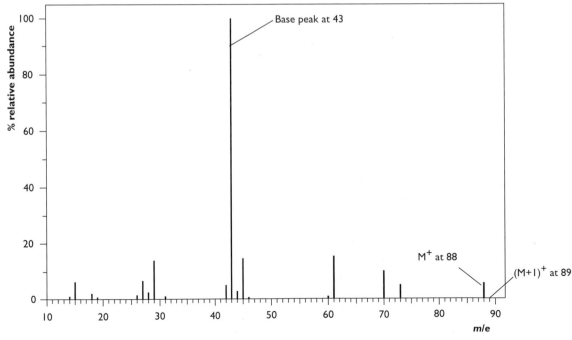

Figure 1

CCEA A2 Chemistry

Explanation of the spectrum

- The molecular ion (M^+) peak is at the m/e value of 88 and the species responsible is $CH_3COOCH_2CH_3^+$.
- The $(M+1)^+$ peak is at an m/e value of 89 and is caused by one ^{13}C atom in the molecule. The species responsible for this peak can be represented by $^{13}CH_3COOCH_2CH_3^+$ but the ^{13}C could be any one of the carbon atoms in the parent molecule.
- The most stable ion is the species causing the peak at an m/e value of 43 (base peak) and the species responsible is represented by CH_3CO^+.
- The RMM of the compound is 88 as the molecular ion (M^+) is found at an m/e value of 88.
- Other major peaks, and the species responsible, are:
  - $m/e = 29$ species = $CH_3CH_2^+$ (or $C_2H_5^+$)
  - $m/e = 45$ species = $CH_3CH_2O^+$ (or $C_2H_5O^+$)
- The pattern for m/e values below the molecular ion peak at 88 is caused by the molecule fragmenting during the vaporisation and ionisation. The pattern is called the **fragmentation pattern** and is unique to a particular molecule.
- There is no peak at $(M+2)^+$ so no Cl or Br atom is present.
- Often there is a peak at the m/e value 1 unit less than the RMM of the compound as the compound loses one hydrogen atom. This is called the $(M-1)^+$ peak.
- There is a small $(M-1)^+$ peak in the spectrum of ethyl ethanoate.

Fragmentation pattern

All peaks below the molecular ion peak are caused by fragmentation of the molecule. The process of mass spectrometry is extremely disruptive and will break the molecule apart, breaking the covalent bonds and creating fragment ions of the molecule. The spectrum in Figure 2 is that of ethanol:

Examiner tip
Mass numbers are only included when the most common isotope of the element is not present. For the $(M+1)^+$ peak, the species responsible can have any one carbon atom as a ^{13}C.

Examiner tip
If you are unsure about what species causes a fragment, break up the molecule by breaking any C–C bonds and work out the RMM of the fragments created.

Examiner tip
When asked what species causes a peak, always remember to include a single positive charge on the ion.

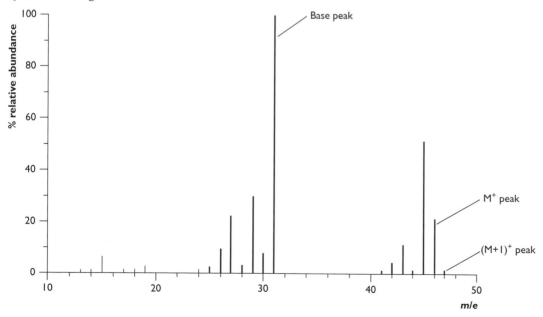

Figure 2

The molecular ion is not the most stable ion formed. The most stable ion is the base peak ion, which in the spectrum of ethanol is at an *m/e* value of 31.

The molecular ion peak is $C_2H_5OH^+$ (the + charge is essential when identifying a peak).

The structure of ethanol is shown in Figure 3.

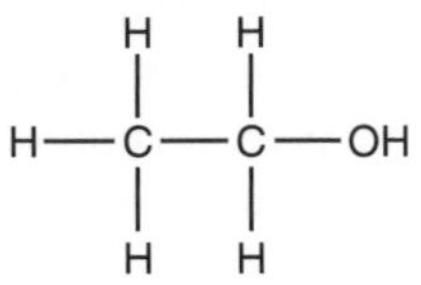

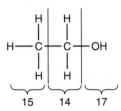

Figure 3

Identifying peaks in the spectrum

When working out which species is responsible for the peak at 31, check the mass of the individual parts of the ethanol molecule. C–H bonds are usually the last to be broken. Major fragments of the molecule are shown in Figure 4.

Figure 4

The fragments can be considered independently and therefore we would expect peaks at *m/e* ratios of 15, 14 and 17, which are small peaks but are still present.
- The peak at *m/e* 31 is the base peak. It is caused by the ion CH_2OH^+.
- The peak at *m/e* 29 is caused by the ion $CH_3CH_2^+$.
- The peak at *m/e* 15 is caused by the ion CH_3^+.
- The peak at *m/e* 14 is caused by the ion CH_2^+.
- The peak at *m/e* 17 is caused by the ion OH^+.

For larger molecules, the identity of a species that causes a peak in a spectrum can be determined by calculating the mass that has been lost from the molecular ion. For example, the peak at *m/e* 31 (the base peak) shows a difference of 15 from the RMM of the molecule (46 − 31 = 15). The part of the molecule responsible for a mass of 15 has to be CH_3. This would mean that the molecule has lost CH_3, hence leaving the ion CH_2OH^+.

Compounds containing chlorine and bromine

The mass spectrum of chloroethane is shown in Figure 5, with some labels to indicate the main peaks.

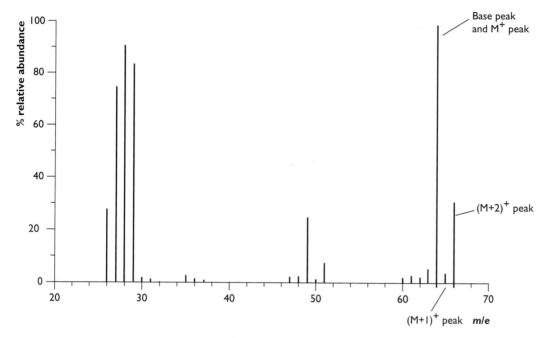

Figure 5

For chlorine- or bromine-containing molecules it is important to remember that both of these elements have isotopes that differ by two mass units:
- Cl ^{35}CI and ^{37}CI 75% ^{35}CI and 25% ^{37}CI
- Br ^{79}Br and ^{81}Br 50% ^{79}Br and 50% ^{81}Br

The presence of a chlorine atom or a bromine atom will result in a peak at $(M+2)^+$. If the M^+ peak is three times as abundant as the $(M+2)^+$ peak, this indicates the presence of a Cl atom. If the M^+ peak has the same abundance as the $(M+2)^+$ peak, this indicates the presence of a Br atom.

The M^+ peak and also the base peak occur at an m/e value of 64. This is for the molecular ion $CH_3CH_2{}^{35}CI^+$.

The spectrum for chloroethane indicates an $(M+1)^+$ peak that is caused by a species containing ^{35}Cl and one ^{13}C atom. The $(M+2)^+$ peak is caused by the presence of ^{37}CI in a molecule. Hence the $(M+2)^+$ peak is caused by $CH_3CH_2{}^{37}CI^+$.

Fragments occur at the m/e values of 51, 49, 29, 28, 27, 26. These are caused by the following ions:
- 51 $CH_2{}^{37}CI^+$
- 49 $CH_2{}^{35}CI^+$
- 29 $CH_3CH_2{}^+$
- 28 CH_3CH^+
- 27 CH_3C^+ or CH_2CH^+
- 26 CH_2C^+ or $CHCH^+$

Unknown mass spectrum

Sometimes the composition by mass of a compound may be given and you will be asked to determine the empirical formula of the compound.

Worked example

An organic compound contains 68.9% carbon, 4.9% hydrogen and 26.2% oxygen by mass. Determine its empirical formula and use the mass spectrum in Figure 6 to determine a possible identity of the compound.

	C	H	O
Mass	68.9 g	4.9 g	26.2 g
Moles	$\frac{68.9}{12} = 5.74$	$\frac{4.9}{1} = 4.9$	$\frac{26.2}{16} = 1.64$
Ratio (1.64 = 1)	3.5	3	1
Empirical ratio	7	6	2
Empirical formula = $C_7H_6O_2$			

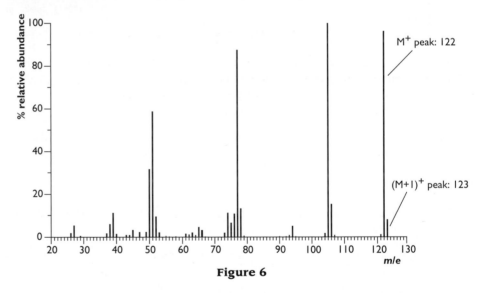

Figure 6

The mass spectrum can provide a great deal of information about the molecule, including its identity, from a relatively simple analysis:

- The absence of an $(M+2)^+$ peak agrees with the fact that the molecule does not contain a halogen atom.
- The RMM of the molecule is 122.
- There is the possibility that it is a molecule containing a benzene ring. Peaks around 72 to 77 would provide more evidence for the presence of a benzene ring. Benzene has an RMM of 78 but a substituted benzene ring would have fewer hydrogen atoms. A large peak at an m/e value of 77 is caused by the $C_6H_5^+$ ion.
- The fact that the fragmentation pattern peaks below 72 are small would also indicate a benzene ring because it is more stable and not disrupted as easily as an aliphatic (straight-chain) molecule.

- The removal of C_6H_5 from the empirical formula would leave CHO_2 or $COOH$, which would possibly suggest benzoic acid C_6H_5COOH. Esters are isomeric with carboxylic acids so phenyl methanoate, $HCOOC_6H_5$, is another possibility.
- The RMMs of benzoic acid and phenyl ethanoate are 122, which are the same as the m/e value for M^+ peak.
- Benzoic acid will always give the same fragmentation pattern under the same conditions and so comparison with known spectra can identify the molecule.

High-resolution mass spectrometry

We have been looking at low-resolution mass spectrometry where the mass of the atoms is not measured very accurately. In high-resolution mass spectrometry, the mass of the atoms is measured much more accurately *to many decimal places* and this enables peaks to be identified without any ambiguity.

A peak at an m/e value of 28 on a low-resolution mass spectrum could be caused by one of the following ions: $C_2H_4^+$, CO^+. However, with high-resolution mass spectrometry this problem is eliminated as the mass of the atoms is measured very accurately:

- C   12.00000
- O   15.99491
- H   1.007825

Using high-resolution mass spectrometry a peak found at an m/e value of 28.03130 can only be caused by $C_2H_4^+$, as the following calculations show:

- $C_2H_4^+$ 28.03130
- CO^+ 27.99491

Mass spectrometry–gas-liquid chromatography (MS–GLC or GLC–MS)

Gas-liquid chromatography provides an efficient method for separating components of a mixture. These components can then be fed directly into a mass spectrometer. This enables better and clearer identification of the components rather than the mixed signal obtained when just mass spectrometry is used on its own.

A complex mixture can be separated into all (or most) of its components by GLC and each component can then be analysed using mass spectrometry. This allows for powerful analysis of complex samples, including many biological samples such as amino acids, lipids and carbohydrates. Cow muscle and human blood plasma can be analysed in this way.

Figure 7 shows GLC apparatus linked to a mass spectrometer. The data obtained would be analysed by computer to identify the components of the mixture based on their spectra in a database.

Examiner tip
An analysis of the functional groups present by IR spectroscopy would identify the —OH group and C==O group of an acid. Often mass spectra, IR spectra and nmr spectra are given together to enable complete identification of the molecule. One type of spectrum can give a suggestion but all three can be used to identify the molecule completely without comparison to a database for one analytical technique.

Examiner tip
High-resolution mass spectrometry removes the ambiguity about peak identification that can exist at low resolution and allows for very accurate measurement of relative atomic masses.

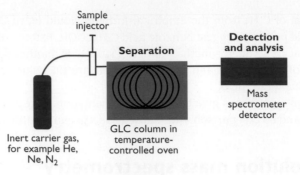

Figure 7

Using mass spectrometry to determine mechanism

Example: esterification

The production of the ester ethyl ethanoate involves the elimination of a water molecule (Figure 8). The reaction could occur in one of two ways:

- The water molecule can be formed from the OH on the alcohol and the H on the carboxylic acid. This would mean the ester would contain the O atom from the acid.
- The water molecule can be formed from the H on the alcohol and the OH on the carboxylic acid. This would mean the ester would contain the O atom from the alcohol.

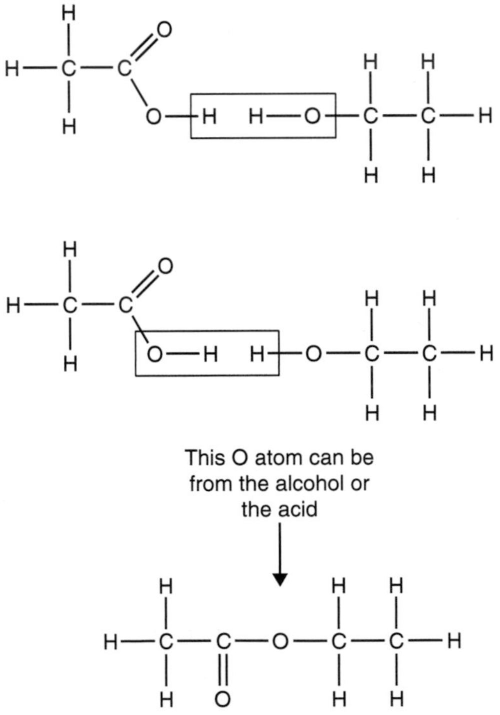

Figure 8

The origin of the O atom can be determined by isotopic labelling of the O atom on the alcohol. ^{18}O is incorporated into the alcohol molecule. This can be achieved by producing water using H_2 and $^{18}O_2$. The labelled water is reacted with ethene to produce $CH_3CH_2^{18}OH$.

Ethanoic acid and the labelled ethanol are used to prepare a pure sample of the ester and the ester is subjected to mass spectrometry. The mass spectrum is analysed to look for the molecular ion peak that would normally be at an m/e value of 88. If the peak still occurs at this value, then the oxygen atom in the ester comes from the acid. If the molecular ion peak occurs at an m/e value of 90, then the oxygen atom in the cstcr is from the alcohol.

The main purpose of isotopic labelling and mass spectrometry is to follow the movement of a particular atom and hence determine the mechanism of the reaction. In the mass spectrum of the ester, the M^+ peak does occur at an m/e value of 90, so the oxygen atom in the ester originally comes from the alcohol.

- All ions in a mass spectrum are considered to have a charge of 1+.
- The vertical axis of a mass spectrum is relative abundance or % relative abundance; the horizontal axis is mass, usually given as m/e or m/z.
- The molecular ion peak in the mass spectrum of a compound is the major peak at the highest m/e value.
- The base peak is the peak in the spectrum with the highest relative abundance.
- The $(M+1)^+$ peak is the peak where the species contains one ^{13}C atom.
- The presence of an $(M+2)^+$ peak indicates the presence of a chlorine or bromine atom in the molecule.

Summary

Nuclear magnetic resonance spectroscopy

Nuclear magnetic resonance (nmr) spectroscopy is the process where a compound is analysed for its ^1H atoms. The sample is compared with a standard — tetramethylsilane, $Si(CH_3)_4$ — which is often written as TMS. Chemically equivalent hydrogen atoms are all in the same chemical environment and appear at the same chemical shift on an nmr spectrum. All the hydrogen atoms in tetramethylsilane are chemically equivalent. A ^1H atom bonded in an organic compound has its nucleus exposed (as the electron from the hydrogen atom is in the covalent bond).

The nucleus is spinning and creating a magnetic moment. The further away the bonded electrons are from the proton (caused by being attached to an electronegative atom like N or O), the more deshielded the proton. A proton is described as deshielded when the electrons in the bond are further away from it. Other hydrogen nuclei (protons) that are neighbouring (i.e. attached to the next carbon atom) will split the signal on a high resolution nmr spectrum.

Knowledge check 2

What are chemically equivalent hydrogen atoms?

Features of an nmr spectrum

- The horizontal axis is chemical shift, represented by the Greek letter δ (delta). It has units of parts per million (ppm) and it runs from right to left.
- The vertical axis is most often not labelled or labelled signal intensity.
- The peak at δ = 0 is caused by tetramethylsilane (TMS). TMS is used as a standard.

Examiner tip

All the hydrogen atoms in one peak (or one set of peaks) are chemically equivalent. Chemically equivalent hydrogen atoms occur at the same chemical shift on an nmr spectrum.

Examiner tip

The heights of the peaks when split are based on Pascal's triangle:
- for a doublet they should be roughly the same height, 1:1
- for a triplet they should be in the height ratio 1:2:1
- for a quartet they should be in the height ratio 1:3:3:1
- for a quintet they should be in the height ratio 1:4:6:4:1

Examiner tip

A CH_3CH_2 (ethyl) group is common in organic chemistry and gives a characteristic splitting pattern of a triplet and a quartet.

Knowledge check 3

What does TMS stand for and what is it used for in nmr spectroscopy?

- The number of peaks (or sets of peaks) identifies the number of different types of chemical environments of ^1H atoms.
- The area under each peak is equivalent to the ratio of the number of hydrogen atoms in each chemical environment. An integration trace can be given to indicate the ratio of hydrogen atoms in each chemical environment.
- The spin–spin splitting pattern is caused by hydrogen atoms bonded to adjacent carbon atoms. This depends on the $n+1$ rule. If there are two hydrogen atoms bonded to adjacent carbon atoms, then the peak is split into 3. If there are 0 hydrogen atoms bonded to adjacent carbon atoms, then the peak is not split (i.e. 1 peak).
- The group of peaks created by splitting is called:
  - a singlet if it is not split at all (i.e. one peak)
  - a doublet if it is split into two peaks
  - a triplet if it is split into three peaks
  - a quartet if it is split into four peaks
  - a quintet if it is split into five peaks
  and so on.
- Low-resolution nmr does not show the splitting pattern; high-resolution nmr (the one normally used) shows splitting if it is present.
- Hydrogen atoms attached to electronegative atoms or attached to carbon atoms that are attached to electronegative atoms are deshielded and appear more downfield (at a higher chemical shift value).
- Hydrogen atoms in alkyl groups with no electronegative atoms close by are less deshielded and appear more upfield (at lower chemical shift values).

Example of an nmr spectrum

Figure 9 shows an example of an nmr spectrum.

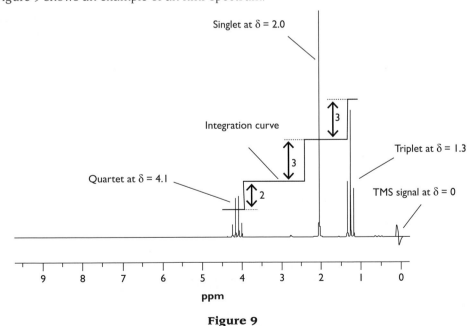

Figure 9

CCEA A2 Chemistry

Explanation of the nmr spectrum

- The peak at $\delta = 0$ is due to the chemically equivalent hydrogen atoms in TMS.
- There are three different chemical environments of hydrogen atoms represented by the three sets of peaks.
- The height differences in the integration curve as shown give the ratio of hydrogen atoms in each environment — 3:3:2 from right to left.
- The triplet at $\delta = 1.3$ represents three hydrogen atoms. As there are three peaks in the set, they have two hydrogen atoms bonded to adjacent carbon atom(s) — probably a CH_3 with a CH_2 neighbouring.
- The singlet at $\delta = 2.0$ represents three hydrogen atoms. As there is a single peak, there are no hydrogen atoms bonded to adjacent carbon atom(s). This represents a CH_3 with no hydrogen atoms neighbouring.
- The quartet at $\delta = 4.1$ represents two hydrogen atoms. As there are four peaks, there are three neighbouring hydrogen atoms bonded to adjacent carbon atom(s). This probably represents a CH_2 with a CH_3 neighbouring.
- The presence of the peaks at $\delta = 1.3$ and $\delta = 4.1$ would suggest the presence of a CH_3CH_2 group.
- The fact that the quartet at $\delta = 4.1$ is deshielded more than would be expected would suggest the CH_2 is close to an electronegative element such as oxygen.
- The chemically equivalent environments for ethyl ethanoate are as follows:

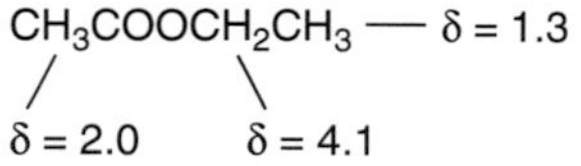

$$CH_3COOCH_2CH_3 \longrightarrow \delta = 1.3$$
$$\swarrow \qquad \searrow$$
$$\delta = 2.0 \qquad \delta = 4.1$$

Examiner tip
Often nmr spectrum questions give a spectrum with a molecular formula and expect an analysis based on chemical shift (different environments of chemically equivalent hydrogen atoms), peak integration (number of hydrogen atoms in each environment) and spin–spin splitting (which identifies the number of hydrogen atoms bonded to adjacent carbon atoms).

- Chemically equivalent hydrogen atoms are at the same chemical shift (δ) on an nmr spectrum.
- The number of hydrogen atoms bonded to adjacent carbon atoms is governed by the $n+1$ rule, where $n+1$ is the number of split peaks for n hydrogen atoms bonded to adjacent carbon atoms.
- If a hydrogen atom is in close proximity to an electronegative element such as oxygen or nitrogen, it will be more deshielded in an nmr spectrum
- The peak integration (area under the peaks) gives the ratio of the number of hydrogen atoms in each environment.

Summary

Volumetric analysis

Edta titrations

Edta (**e**thylene**d**iamine**t**etr**a**acetic acid) is usually written as the anion edta^{4-}. Edta complexes formed with metal ions are stable. Metal ions react with edta in a 1:1 ratio.

The structure of edta is shown in Figure 10.

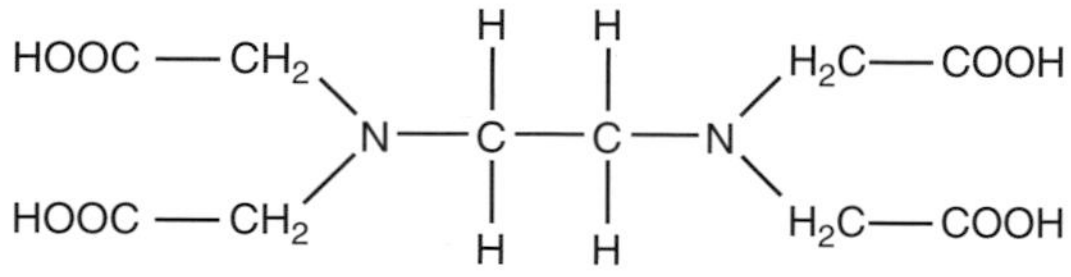

Examiner tip
You should revise the content of Titrations in AS Unit 1 to ensure that you are aware of the practical details of how to prepare apparatus for use in a titration, prepare and dilute solutions and carry out the titration, including the recording of results.

$$HOOC-CH_2 \diagdown \qquad \overset{H}{\underset{H}{\overset{|}{C}}}-\overset{H}{\underset{H}{\overset{|}{C}}} \diagup H_2C-COOH$$

N—C—C—N

HOOC—CH₂   H₂C—COOH

Figure 10 Structure of edta

In titrations, edta should be kept in the form of the anion, so edta solutions are made up in alkaline (usually pH 10) buffers or pH 10 buffer may be added to the metal ion solution in the conical flask.

The edta^{4-} anion present in alkaline solution is shown in Figure 11. Edta is a hexadentate ligand (see page 35); the attachment points are labelled 1 to 6.

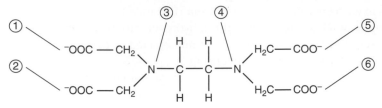

Figure 11 Attachment points for edta^{4-}

Mg^{2+} and Ca^{2+} determination

Mg^{2+} and Ca^{2+} ions in solution can be estimated in a titration with edta. The edta reacts with the metal ion to form a complex:

$$[Mg(H_2O)_6]^{2+} + edta^{4-} \rightleftharpoons [Mg(edta)]^{2-} + 6H_2O$$

This equation can be written more simply as:

$$Mg^{2+} + edta^{4-} \rightleftharpoons [Mg(edta)]^{2-}$$

The solutions must be buffered at pH 10. The indicator for the titration is eriochrome black T (sometimes called solochrome black). The free indicator is blue but it complexes with Mg^{2+} to form a red solution. Ligand replacement occurs during the titration and the edta^{4-} replaces the eriochrome black T in the complex. The Mg^{2+}/Ca^{2+}–indicator complex is red. When only [Mg(edta)]$^{2-}$ or [Ca(edta)]$^{2-}$ is present the free indicator is completely released and it is blue. *The colour change at the end point is red to blue.*

Method of analysis

A typical method of carrying out an edta titration is given below, with practical details.

1 Pipette 25.0 cm³ of the solution containing Mg^{2+} ions or Ca^{2+} ions into a conical flask. Add pH 10 buffer to the solution in the conical flask.
   The solution must be buffered at pH 10 to maintain the edta^{4-} in this form; edta^{4-} can form six coordinate bonds with the metal ion.

2 Add a few granules of eriochrome black T from the tip of a spatula or a few drops of a solution of eriochrome black T; the solution changes to red.
   A solution of eriochrome black T made up in a pH 10 buffer can be used as the indicator or the solid indicator can be added. Add a small amount, as it is easier to add more indicator and impossible to remove excess. A very dark red and a very dark blue can both appear black.

3 Titrate with a **standard solution** of edta solution until the indicator changes from red to blue.
   The solution of edta may also be buffered at pH 10. A colour reference solution for the blue colour at the end point may be provided.

4 Carry out one rough titration and two accurate titrations with standard edta solution and calculate an average titre using the two accurate titration values.

Edta titration calculations

These calculations are generally straightforward as the ratio of edta to the metal cation is 1:1.

$$\text{moles of edta added} = \frac{\text{volume} \times \text{concentration}}{1000} = a$$

moles of Mg^{2+} or Ca^{2+} in volume of solution used in titration (usually 25 cm³) = a

As the ratio of metal ion to edta is 1:1:

$$\text{concentration of } Mg^{2+} \text{ or } Ca^{2+} = \frac{a}{\text{volume used in titration}} \times 1000$$

If a dilution has been carried out, then multiply this concentration by the dilution factor.

Worked example

A solution of calcium chloride was diluted by placing 25.0 cm³ in a volumetric flask and making up the volume to 250.0 cm³ using deionised water. 25.0 cm³ of the diluted solution were placed in a conical flask and a pH 10 buffer and the indicator eriochrome black T were added. The solution was titrated against 0.05 mol dm⁻³ edta solution. The procedure is shown in Figure 12.

The average titre was determined to be 12.7 cm³. Calculate the concentration of the original solution of calcium chloride in g dm⁻³.

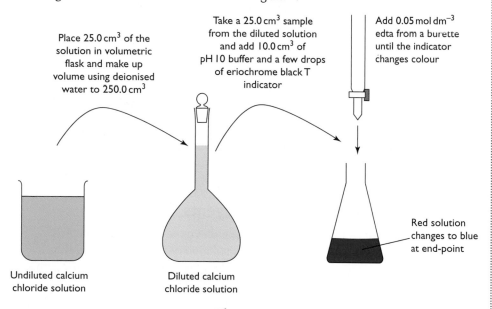

Place 25.0 cm³ of the solution in volumetric flask and make up volume using deionised water to 250.0 cm³

Take a 25.0 cm³ sample from the diluted solution and add 10.0 cm³ of pH 10 buffer and a few drops of eriochrome black T indicator

Add 0.05 mol dm⁻³ edta from a burette until the indicator changes colour

Red solution changes to blue at end-point

Undiluted calcium chloride solution

Diluted calcium chloride solution

Figure 12

The calculation at A2 is often more open-ended, with you using your knowledge to work through the various stages.

$$\text{moles of edta used} = \frac{\text{volume} \times \text{concentration}}{1000}$$

$$= \frac{12.7 \times 0.05}{1000} = 0.000635\,\text{mol}$$

moles of Ca^{2+} in $25.0\,cm^3$ of diluted solution = $0.000635\,mol$

1:1 ratio of edta to metal ion.

concentration of diluted $CaCl_2$ solution = $0.00635 \times 40 = 0.0254\,mol\,dm^{-3}$

×40 is the same as dividing by 25 and multiplying by 1000 so converting to per dm³ from 25 cm³.

concentration of undiluted $CaCl_2$ solution = $0.254\,mol\,dm^{-3}$

Dilution factor is ×10, so can multiply by 10 to calculate the concentration of the undiluted solution.

concentration of undiluted $CaCl_2$ solution in $g\,dm^{-3}$ = 0.254×111
$$= 28.194\,g\,dm^{-3}$$

The RFM of $CaCl_2$ is 111.

Iodine–thiosulfate titrations

Iodine–thiosulfate titrations are used to determine the concentration of an oxidising agent.

1 A known volume (usually $25.0\,cm^3$) of a solution of the oxidising agent is placed in a conical flask.
2 The mixture is acidified using an excess of sulfuric acid.
3 Solid excess potassium iodide is added.
4 Iodine in solution in the conical flask is titrated with standard sodium thiosulfate solution.

The brown colour of the mixture fades to yellow; when a straw colour is reached a few drops of starch indicator are added; the titration is continued until the blue-black colour of the indicator changes to colourless.

Common examples of oxidising agents

- iodate(v) ions, IO_3^- — for example, sodium iodate(v) or potassium iodate(v)
- hydrogen peroxide, H_2O_2 — for example, a solution of hydrogen peroxide

Remember that the oxidising agent is reduced and oxidises the iodide to iodine.

Knowledge check 4

State the colour change observed at the end-point in an edta titration.

An **oxidising agent** (or oxidant) is an electron acceptor.

Examiner tip

The reaction between the oxidising agent and iodide ions requires the presence of hydrogen ions, which the sulfuric acid provides. The sulfur in sulfuric acid is in its highest oxidation state, so cannot be oxidised any further by the oxidising agent.

Examiner tip

The oxidising agent oxidises iodide to iodine — the solution changes from colourless to brown. Excess potassium iodide is used to ensure that all the oxidising agent reacts.

CCEA A2 Chemistry

Iodate(v) ions

Iodate(v) ions reduction:

$$2IO_3^- + 12H^+ + 10e^- \rightarrow I_2 + 6H_2O$$

Oxidation state of I = +5   Oxidation state of I = 0

Iodide ions oxidation: $2I^- \rightarrow I_2 + 2e^-$

Combining equations: $2IO_3^- + 12H^+ + 10e^- \rightarrow I_2 + 6H_2O$

$2I^- \rightarrow I_2 + 2e^-$ (×5 to balance electrons)

$2IO_3^- + 12H^+ + 10e^- \rightarrow I_2 + 6H_2O$

$10I^- \rightarrow 5I_2 + 10e^-$

Ionic equation: $2IO_3^- + 12H^+ + 10I^- \rightarrow 6I_2 + 6H_2O$

or $IO_3^- + 6H^+ + 5I^- \rightarrow 3I_2 + 3H_2O$

The most important part of the above equation is to realise that 1 mol of iodate(v) ions, IO_3^-, produces 3 mol of iodine, I_2, when 1 mol of iodate(v) ions reacts with excess iodide ions in the presence of H^+ ions.

Hydrogen peroxide

Hydrogen peroxide reduction:

$$H_2O_2 + 2H^+ + 2e^- \rightarrow 2H_2O$$

Iodide ions oxidation: $2I^- \rightarrow I_2 + 2e^-$

Combining equations: $H_2O_2 + 2H^+ + 2e^- \rightarrow 2H_2O$

$2I^- \rightarrow I_2 + 2e^-$ (both 2e⁻ so just add equations to cancel e⁻)

Ionic equation: $H_2O_2 + 2I^- + 2H^+ \rightarrow 2H_2O + I_2$

The most important part of the above equation is to realise that 1 mol of hydrogen peroxide, H_2O_2, produces 1 mol of iodine, I_2, when 1 mol of hydrogen peroxide reacts with excess iodide ions in the presence of H^+ ions.

Examiner tip

If you can work out oxidation numbers you can work out this half equation. The iodine in IO_3^- is reduced from +5 to 0 in I_2. In the zero oxidation state iodine is diatomic, so the equation is balanced by placing 2 before the IO_3^-. Hydrogen ions are required (this is why sulfuric acid is added) and electrons are required on the left-hand side as it is a reduction. Balance the charges.

Knowledge check 5

Write a balanced symbol equation for the reaction of potassium iodate(v) with potassium iodide in the presence of sulfuric acid.

Examiner tip

Learn the hydrogen peroxide half equation or be able to work it out. The hydrogen peroxide in acidic solution (H^+ ions present) is reduced (gains electrons) to water. The charges in the equation must balance (each side must have the same overall charge).

The iodine produced in these reactions is titrated with sodium thiosulfate solution. The iodine reacts with the thiosulfate ions according to the equation:

$$I_2 + 2S_2O_3^{2-} \rightarrow 2I^- + S_4O_6^{2-}$$

Overall ratios

When iodate(v) ions, IO_3^-, are used the ratio of $IO_3^-:I_2$ is 1:3.

When hydrogen peroxide, H_2O_2, is used the ratio of $H_2O_2:I_2$ is 1:1.

This type of titration is slightly more complex as the oxidising agent oxidises the iodide ions to iodine in the conical flask. Then the iodine that has been produced in the conical flask is titrated using sodium thiosulfate solution (see Figure 13).

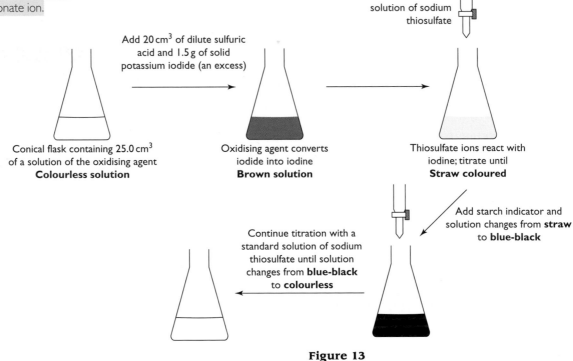

Figure 13

Worked example

A solid sample of sodium iodate(v), $NaIO_3$, was dissolved in water and transferred to a 250 cm³ volumetric flask and the volume made up to 250.0 cm³ using deionised water (Figure 14).

25.0 cm³ of this solution were placed in a conical flask. 20 cm³ of dilute sulfuric acid were added and 2 g of solid potassium iodide (an excess). The resulting solution was titrated with 0.1 mol dm⁻³ sodium thiosulfate solution and the average titre was determined to be 17.5 cm³. Calculate the mass of sodium iodate(v) used to make the original solution.

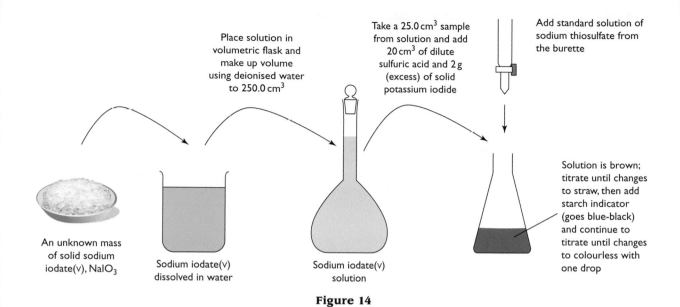

Figure 14

$$\text{moles of sodium thiosulfate used} = \frac{\text{volume} \times \text{concentration}}{1000} = \frac{17.5 \times 0.1}{1000}$$
$$= 0.00175\,\text{mol}$$

Remember that this is the same as the number of moles of thiosulfate ions because 1 mol of $Na_2S_2O_3$ contains 1 mol of thiosulfate ions, $S_2O_3^{2-}$.

In the equation, the ratio of $I_2:S_2O_3^{2-}$ is 1:2. So:

$$\text{moles of } I_2 \text{ in conical flask} = \frac{0.00175}{2} = 0.000875\,\text{mol}$$

In the equation, the ratio of $IO_3^-:I_2$ is 1:3. So:

$$\text{moles of } IO_3^- \text{ in 25.0 cm}^3 \text{ in conical flask} = \frac{0.000875}{3} = 0.000292\,\text{mol}$$

moles of IO_3^- in 250 cm³ in volumetric flask = $0.000292 \times 10 = 0.00292\,\text{mol}$

moles of $NaIO_3$ used = $0.00292\,\text{mol}$

mass of $NaIO_3$ used = $0.00292 \times 198 = 0.578\,\text{g}$

RFM of NaIO₃ = 198

Knowledge check 6

What is the colour change observed at the end-point of an iodine–thiosulfate titration?

Potassium manganate(VII) titrations

Potassium manganate(VII) (or potassium permanganate) has the formula $KMnO_4$ and is a purple solid, which forms a purple solution. Manganate(VII) ions are MnO_4^-.

Purple potassium manganate(VII) is easily reduced to pale pink (virtually colourless) manganese(II) ions according to the equation:

$$MnO_4^- \quad + \quad 8H^+ \quad + \quad 5e^- \quad \rightarrow \quad Mn^{2+} \quad + \quad 4H_2O$$

$\downarrow$ $\downarrow$

Oxidation state of Mn is +7   Oxidation state of Mn is +2

Examiner tip

You should know this half-equation from AS Unit 1 and again should be able to work it out using oxidation numbers.

A **reducing agent** (or reductant) is an electron donor.

Potassium manganate(VII) can be used to determine the concentration of **reducing agents** in two ways:

- Direct titration
  1. $25.0\,cm^3$ of a solution of the reducing agent is placed in a conical flask.
  2. The mixture is acidified using excess dilute sulfuric acid.
  3. The standard solution of potassium manganate(VII) is added from the burette until the solution changes from colourless to pink.

- Titration with iron(II) ions in solution produced from reduction of iron(III) ions

  1. A known amount (volume and concentration or mass) of a reducing agent is added to a known volume and concentration of a solution containing iron(III) ions which are in excess.

The reducing agent reduces some of the iron(III) to iron(II).

  2. Place a known volume (usually $25.0\,cm^3$) of the reduced solution in a conical flask.
  3. Acidify the solution with excess dilute sulfuric acid.
  4. The standard solution of potassium manganate(VII) is added from the burette until the solution changes from colourless to pink.

Common examples of reducing agents

- iron(II) ions, Fe^{2+} — for example, iron(II) sulfate and ammonium iron(II) sulfate
- oxalate ions, $C_2O_4^{2-}$ — for example, sodium oxalate and potassium oxalate

Iron(II) ions

Manganate(VII) ions reduction: $MnO_4^- + 8H^+ + 5e^- \rightarrow Mn^{2+} + 4H_2O$

Iron(II) ions oxidation: $Fe^{2+} \rightarrow Fe^{3+} + e^-$

Combining equations: $MnO_4^- + 8H^+ + 5e^- \rightarrow Mn^{2+} + 4H_2O$

$Fe^{2+} \rightarrow Fe^{3+} + e^-$ (×5 to cancel electrons)

$MnO_4^- + 8H^+ + 5e^- \rightarrow Mn^{2+} + 4H_2O$

$5Fe^{2+} \rightarrow 5Fe^{3+} + 5e^-$

Ionic equation: $MnO_4^- + 8H^+ + 5Fe^{2+} \rightarrow Mn^{2+} + 5Fe^{3+} + 4H_2O$

Oxalate ions, $C_2O_4^{2-}$

Manganate(VII) ions reduction: $MnO_4^- + 8H^+ + 5e^- \rightarrow Mn^{2+} + 4H_2O$

Oxalate ions oxidation: $C_2O_4^{2-} \rightarrow 2CO_2 + 2e^-$

Combining equations: $MnO_4^- + 8H^+ + 5e^- \rightarrow Mn^{2+} + 4H_2O$ (×2)

$C_2O_4^{2-} \rightarrow 2CO_2 + 2e^-$ (×5)

$2MnO_4^- + 16H^+ + 10e^- \rightarrow 2Mn^{2+} + 8H_2O$

$5C_2O_4^{2-} \rightarrow 10CO_2 + 10e^-$

Ionic equation: $2MnO_4^- + 16H^+ + 5C_2O_4^{2-} \rightarrow 2Mn^{2+} + 10CO_2 + 8H_2O$

> **Examiner tip**
> The most important thing here is to realise that 2 mol of manganate(VII) ions, MnO_4^-, react with 5 mol of oxalate ions, $C_2O_4^{2-}$.

Overall ratios

1 mol of MnO_4^- reacts with 5 mol of Fe^{2+}.

2 mol of MnO_4^- react with 5 mol of $C_2O_4^{2-}$.

Worked example I

1.39 g of a sample of hydrated iron(II) sulfate, $FeSO_4.xH_2O$ were dissolved in dilute sulfuric acid and the volume made up using deionised water to 250.0 cm³ in a volumetric flask. A 25.0 cm³ sample of this solution was acidified and titrated against 0.005 mol dm⁻³ potassium manganate(VII) solution (Figure 15). The average titre was found to be 20.0 cm³. Calculate the degree of hydration of hydrated iron(II) sulfate.

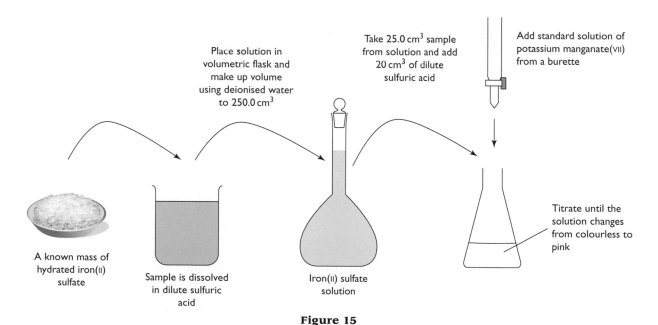

Place solution in volumetric flask and make up volume using deionised water to 250.0 cm³

Take 25.0 cm³ sample from solution and add 20 cm³ of dilute sulfuric acid

Add standard solution of potassium manganate(VII) from a burette

A known mass of hydrated iron(II) sulfate

Sample is dissolved in dilute sulfuric acid

Iron(II) sulfate solution

Titrate until the solution changes from colourless to pink

Figure 15

Examiner tip

Iron(II) sulfate is usually dissolved in dilute sulfuric acid because it is more soluble in dilute sulfuric acid than in water. Solutions in water are often cloudy.

Knowledge check 7

State the colour change observed at the end-point in a manganate(VII) titration.

Examiner tip

Both the RFM and ratio methods were discussed in AS Unit 1.

$$\text{moles of potassium manganate (VII) used} = \frac{\text{volume} \times \text{concentration}}{1000}$$
$$= \frac{20.0 \times 0.005}{1000} = 0.0001 \, \text{mol}$$

In the equation, the ratio of MnO_4^-:Fe^{2+} is 1:5, so:

moles of Fe^{2+} in 25.0 cm³ in conical flask = 0.0001 × 5 = 0.0005 mol

moles of Fe^{2+} in 250 cm³ in volumetric flask = 0.0005 × 10 = 0.005 mol

moles of hydrated iron(II) sulfate used = 0.005 mol

Each mole of hydrated iron(II) sulfate, $FeSO_4.xH_2O$, contains 1 mol of Fe^{2+} ions, so the number of moles of $FeSO_4.xH_2O$ = moles of Fe^{2+}.

There are two ways of finishing the calculation from here:

Method 1: RFM

$$\text{RFM of } FeSO_4.xH_2O = \frac{\text{mass}}{\text{moles}} = \frac{1.39}{0.005} = 278$$

RFM of $FeSO_4$ = 152

RFM due to xH_2O = 278 − 152 = 126

$$x = \frac{126}{18} = 7$$

So the value of x in $FeSO_4.xH_2O$ is 7.

Method 2: ratios

mass of anhydrous $FeSO_4$ in sample = 0.005 × 152 = 0.76 g

mass of water in sample = 1.39 − 0.76 = 0.63 g

$$\text{moles of water} = \frac{\text{mass}}{\text{RFM}} = \frac{0.63}{18} = 0.035 \, \text{mol}$$

ratio of anhydrous $FeSO_4$:H_2O = 0.005:0.035 = 1:7

So x = 7.

Worked example 2

Sulfate(IV) ions (also called sulphite ions) in natural seawater can reduce iron(III) ions to iron(II) ions. A 25.0 cm³ sample of seawater containing sulfate(IV) ions, SO_3^{2-}, is treated with 25.0 cm³ of 0.01 mol dm⁻³ iron(III) chloride solution (an excess).

$$SO_3^{2-} + H_2O + 2Fe^{3+} \rightarrow SO_4^{2-} + 2Fe^{2+} + 2H^+$$

The resulting solution is placed in a conical flask and an excess of dilute sulfuric acid is added. The solution is titrated with 0.001 mol dm⁻³ potassium manganate(VII) solution and 14.8 cm³ of this solution are required.

Calculate the concentration of sulfate(IV) ions in the seawater in mol dm⁻³.

moles of MnO_4^- used $= \dfrac{14.8 \times 0.001}{1000} = 1.48 \times 10^{-5}$ mol

$$MnO_4^- + 8H^+ + 5Fe^{2+} \rightarrow Mn^{2+} + 5Fe^{3+} + 4H_2O$$

moles of $Fe^{2+} = 1.48 \times 10^{-5} \times 5 = 7.4 \times 10^{-5}$ mol

moles of SO_3^{2-} in $25.0\,cm^3 = \dfrac{7.4 \times 10^{-5}}{2} = 3.7 \times 10^{-5}$ mol

concentration of SO_3^{2-} in $mol\,dm^{-3} = 3.7 \times 10^{-5} \times 40 = 1.48 \times 10^{-3}\,mol\,dm^{-3}$

Summary

- The determination of metal ions in solution (Mg^{2+} and Ca^{2+}) can be carried out using edta solution buffered at pH 10 using eriochrome black T indicator.
- The colour change with eriochrome back T is red to blue.
- Oxidising agents in solution are determined using an iodine–thiosulfate titration where the oxidising agent oxidises iodide to iodine.
- The liberated iodine is then titrated using standard sodium thiosulfate solution until straw coloured; starch indicator is added and the titration continued until the colour change observed is blue-black to colourless.
- Reducing agents are determined using a manganate(VII) titration. The titration is self indicating. At the end point the solution changes from colourless to pink.

Colorimetry

Colorimetry is a method of measuring colour intensity in a solution and relating this to the concentration of the coloured substance.

Formula of copper(II) complex with ammonia

To determine the formula of copper(II) complex with ammonia, i.e. the value of x in $[Cu(NH_3)_x(H_2O)_{6-x}]^{2+}$, prepare a set of samples in which the number of moles of Cu^{2+} ions in solution gradually decreases and the number of moles of ammonia gradually increases, but the total volume is constant. Add ammonium sulfate solution, $(NH_4)_2SO_4(aq)$, again keeping the volume constant.

A sample set of results for the colorimetry experiment is given in Table 1.

Table 1

Sample	1	2	3	4	5	6
Volume of 0.1 M CuSO$_4$(aq)	10	8	6	4	2	0
Volume of 0.1 M NH$_3$(aq)	0	2	4	6	8	10
Volume of 1.5 M (NH$_4$)$_2$SO$_4$(aq)	5	5	5	5	5	5

Calibrate the colorimeter using the appropriate filter (red) and a blank solution. Place the samples in a colorimeter with the red filter and measure the **absorbance** of each sample.

Examiner tip
Ammonium sulfate prevents precipitation of $Cu(OH)_2$ by preventing ammonia forming OH^- ions in solution. It moves the equilibrium $NH_3 + H_2O \rightleftharpoons NH_4^+ + OH^-$ to the left because it provides ammonium ions.

Examiner tip
The solution is blue and therefore it absorbs red light, so a red filter is used in the colorimeter. Choose a filter according to the colour that the solution absorbs and measure the absorbance on the colorimeter.

Plot absorbance against composition of Cu^{2+} and NH_3. The maximum absorbance gives the mole ratio of Cu^{2+} to NH_3 in the complex.

The graph of absorbance against concentration usually looks like the one shown in Figure 16. There should be a clear maximum value of the absorbance.

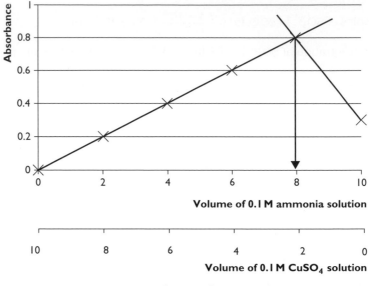

Figure 16

The ratio of the number of moles of NH_3 to $CuSO_4$ is determined from the maximum, taking into account the solution volumes and concentrations of the solutions.

$$\text{moles of } Cu^{2+} = \frac{2 \times 0.1}{1000} = 0.0002 \, \text{mol}$$

$$\text{moles of } NH_3 = \frac{8 \times 0.1}{1000} = 0.0008 \, \text{mol}$$

The ratio of the number of moles of Cu^{2+} to NH_3 gives the value of x, i.e. $0.0002 : 0.0008 = 1 : 4$, so $x = 4$

The correct formula is $[Cu(NH_3)_4(H_2O)_2]^{2+}$.

Formula of iron(III) thiocyanate complex using colorimetry

To determine the formula of iron(III) thiocyanate complex using colorimetry, i.e. the value of x in $[Fe(SCN)_x(H_2O)_{6-x}]^{(3-x)}$, the same procedure is carried out and a graph of absorbance is drawn. The solution formed is blood red in this experiment and the filter used is blue.

The $(3-x)$ charge is used this time because the thiocyanate ion (SCN^-) has a negative charge. The complex is octahedral.

The value of x is determined to be 1 since the ratio of $Fe^{3+} : SCN^-$ is 1:1 at the maximum absorbance, so the complex has the formula $[Fe(SCN)(H_2O)_5]^{2+}$.

Summary

- The formulae of complexes can be determined using colorimetry.
- The maximum absorbance gives the ratio of the metal ion to the ligand in the complex.
- Common complexes determined using this method are $[Cu(NH_3)_4(H_2O)_2]^{2+}$ and $[Fe(H_2O)_5SCN]^{2+}$.

Chromatography

Chromatography is a method of separating mixtures of soluble substances, such as a mixture of amino acids or a mixture of dyes.

In any chromatography process there is a stationary phase and a mobile phase. The components of the mixture dissolve in the mobile phase and move through the stationary phase. The stationary phase can be a solid or a liquid (often supported on a solid). The mobile phase is most often a liquid or a gas. The components in the mixture are separated because they move at different rates as the mobile phase moves.

If the stationary phase is a solid, the components of the mixture may move out of the mobile phase and adsorb onto the surface of the solid stationary phase. The distance they move on a chromatogram depends on how strongly they are adsorbed onto the solid stationary phase. Components that adsorb strongly to the solid stationary phase do not move far and are held back. Components that do not adsorb strongly onto the stationary phase move quickly and much further. This is separation based on adsorption.

If the stationary phase is a liquid, the components in the mixture partition themselves between the mobile phase and the stationary phase depending on their solubility in each. Components that are more soluble in the stationary phase do not move far and are held back. Components that are more soluble in the mobile phase move quickly and much further. This is separation based on partition.

Types of chromatography

The two main types of chromatography using a solid support are:
- paper chromatography — paper is the solid support
- thin-layer chromatography — silica gel is the solid support

Practical method of carrying out paper chromatography/TLC

Running a chromatogram

- Prepare a concentrated solution of the mixture.
- Mark an origin line in pencil (NOT pen) near the bottom of paper/TLC plate and put an X in the middle of the line.
- Apply a concentrated solution to the centre of the X on the pencil line using a capillary tube.

R_f **(retardation factor)**

$$= \frac{\text{distance moved by spot}}{\text{distance moved by solvent}}$$

- Place the paper/TLC plate in the solvent and run until the solvent is close to the top of the paper/TLC plate. (Ensure the solvent remains below the pencil line.)
- Mark the position of the solvent front in pencil and allow the chromatogram to dry.
- Develop using a chemical developing agent or ultraviolet light.
- For amino acids, ninhydrin is used as the chemical developing agent — it stains amino acids purple. If ultraviolet light is used, the spots will be clearly visible. Use a pencil to draw round the spots while under the ultraviolet light.

Analysis of a chromatogram

- Mark the position of the centre of each spot.
- Measure the distance of the centre of the spot from the origin.
- Measure the distance of the solvent front from the origin.
- Calculate the retardation factor (R_f) value for each spot.

Two-way paper chromatography

Two-way paper chromatography allows more definite separation of a complex mixture.

Method

- Prepare a concentrated solution of the mixture.
- Mark an origin line *in pencil* near the bottom of the paper/TLC plate and another at 90° to this first line, as shown in Figure 17.

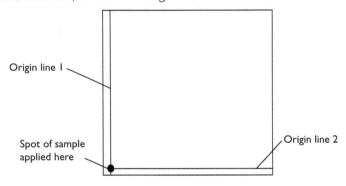

Figure 17

- Apply the concentrated solution of the sample at the intersection of the two pencil lines.
- Place in solvent (name a suitable solvent, for example ethanol) and run until the solvent is close to top of paper. Mark the solvent front in pencil and allow to dry.
- Rotate the chromatogram through 90° and run in a different solvent (again name the solvent, for example propanone) as before.
- Develop the chromatogram using a developing agent/ultraviolet light.

Analysis of a two-way chromatogram

- Mark the position of the centre of each spot on the chromatogram.
- Measure the distance of the centre of the spot from the origin.
- Measure the distance of the solvent front from the origin.

- Calculate the R_f value for each spot in the solvent in the usual way.
- Repeat for the second solvent and determine the second R_f value.

The R_f values of each component should be different in different solvents. This leads to better separation of the components in the mixture than would be achieved using a single solvent.

Gas–liquid chromatography

In gas–liquid chromatography (GLC) the mobile phase is a gas and the stationary phase is a liquid held on a solid support. An inert carrier gas (noble gas or nitrogen) is used as the mobile phase and the gaseous sample is mixed with this gas and injected into a coiled tube (column) in an oven.

The components of the mixture to be separated **partition** themselves between the mobile gas phase and the liquid stationary phase. The more soluble the components are in the stationary liquid phase, the longer they will stay in the coiled column. As the components separate out they come out of the column at different times. The components can be detected and a trace like the one in Figure 18 is produced.

The area under a peak in the detector signal gives a measure of the relative concentration of that component. The number above each peak gives a measure of the area under the curve. The relative concentration of a component can be calculated by dividing the area under a particular peak by the total of the areas for all peaks.

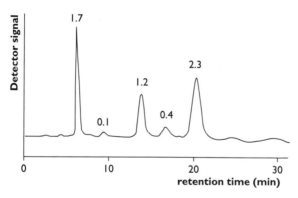

Figure 18

Summary

- Paper chromatography uses paper as the solid support and the solvent as the mobile phase.
- Thin-layer chromatography (TLC) uses a silica paste as the solid support and a solvent as the mobile phase.
- Two-way paper chromatography uses two different solvents with the support rotated through 90° to provided data for the separation in two solvents.
- For paper chromatography and TLC the retardation factor (R_f) is the distance moved by the spot divided by the distance moved by the solvent.
- GLC uses a mobile gas phase and a stationary liquid phase. The retention time is the time between injection of the sample and a component of the sample reaching the detector.

Transition metals

A transition metal is a metal that forms at least one ion with a partially filled d subshell. Scandium and zinc are d block elements but are *not* transition metals.

Transition metals have variable oxidation states. The most common oxidation states of some of the period 4 transition elements are:

- V   +2; +3; +4; +5
- Cr   +3; +6
- Mn   +2; +4; +7
- Fe   +2; +3
- Co   +2; +3
- Ni   +2
- Cu   +1; +2

Catalysis

Transition metals and their compounds can act as catalysts.

Transition metals act as **heterogeneous catalysts** (they are in a different state from the reactants). Make sure you specify the state of the catalyst and the state of the reactants in a reaction.

Transition metal ions in solution can act as homogeneous catalysts (they are in the same state as the reactants).

Examples of heterogeneous transition metal catalysts

- Iron (Fe) in the Haber process:

  $$N_2(g) + 3H_2(g) \rightleftharpoons 2NH_3(g)$$

- Vanadium(v) oxide (V_2O_5) in the contact process:

  $$2SO_2(g) + O_2(g) \rightleftharpoons 2SO_3(g)$$

- Nickel (Ni) in hydrogenation reactions of alkenes and unsaturated fats and oils:

- Platinum/rhodium (Pt/Rh) in the catalytic oxidation of ammonia:

  $$4NH_3(g) + 5O_2(g) \rightleftharpoons 4NO(g) + 6H_2O(g)$$

Ammonia is oxidised using oxygen in the presence of a platinum and rhodium catalyst to form nitrogen monoxide as part of nitric acid manufacture.

Other physical properties

- Transition metals are good conductors of electricity and have high densities.
- Many transition metals form coloured complexes.
- Transition metal ions in aqueous solution are often coloured.
- The aqueous transition metal ions are actually hexaaqua cations. For example, $Ni^{2+}(aq)$ in reality is $[Ni(H_2O)_6]^{2+}(aq)$.

Electronic configuration of transition metals

When writing electronic configurations of transition metal atoms and ions there are a few things to remember:

- The 3*d* fills after the 4*s*.
- The atoms Cr and Cu are unusual in that they have a filled or half-filled 3*d* rather than a filled 4*s*:

Cr atom is: $1s^2, 2s^2, 2p^6, 3s^2, 3p^6, 3d^5, 4s^1$

Cu atom is: $1s^2, 2s^2, 2p^6, 3s^2, 3p^6, 3d^{10}, 4s^1$

- The first series of transition metal atoms lose their 4*s* electrons first when forming ions:

Fe atom is: $1s^2, 2s^2, 2p^6, 3s^2, 3p^6, 3d^6, 4s^2$

Fe^{2+} ion is: $1s^2, 2s^2, 2p^6, 3s^2, 3p^6, 3d^6$

Fe^{3+} ion is: $1s^2, 2s^2, 2p^6, 3s^2, 3p^6, 3d^5$

Chromium

Preparation of potassium dichromate, $K_2Cr_2O_7$

1 Dissolve chromium(III) chloride in 40 cm³ of water.
Observations: green solution

2 Add potassium hydroxide solution to chromium(III) chloride solution until in excess.
Observations: green-blue precipitate, which redissolves to give a deep green solution

3 Slowly add hydrogen peroxide.
4 Heat without boiling.
Observations: green solution changes to yellow

5 Boil the solution for a few minutes.
6 Place in an evaporating basin and add 5 cm³ of glacial ethanoic acid.
Observations: yellow solution changes to orange

7 Heat to concentrate solution and allow to cool and crystallise.
8 Suction-filter off the crystals.
Observations: orange crystals

9 Recrystallise.

Examiner tip

When writing the electronic configuration, make sure you put the 3*d* before the 4*s*. For example, the electronic configuration of manganese is $1s^2, 2s^2, 2p^6, 3s^2, 3p^6, 3d^5, 4s^2$.

Examiner tip

As soon as you start any AS or A2 exam, put an asterisk (*) at Cr and Cu on your periodic table to remind you that their electronic configurations are different from what you would expect.

Knowledge check 10

What is the electronic configuration of an Fe^{2+} ion?

Examiner tip

Chromium(III) ions in solution, as $[Cr(H_2O)_6]^{3+}(aq)$, are violet. Chromium(III) chloride is the most commonly used compound. Ligand replacement means that the solution of this compound is green due to the presence of $[Cr(H_2O)_5Cl]^{2+}(aq)$. CCEA GCE Chemistry states the colour of $Cr^{3+}(aq)$ as green, so make sure you give this as the colour of aqueous Cr^{3+} ions.

Preparation of chrome alum

1 Add a spatula measure of potassium dichromate(VI), $K_2Cr_2O_7$, to water in a test tube and warm the tube until the crystals have dissolved. Cool the solution back to room temperature.

Observations: orange solution formed

2 Add concentrated sulfuric acid dropwise and again cool the solution back to room temperature.

3 Add ethanol slowly while keeping the tube as cold as possible in water. (Note the apple smell of ethanal; the boiling point of ethanal is 21°C.)

4 Pour the solution obtained into a small beaker or crystallising basin and allow it to crystallise in a cool place. (Crystals cannot be obtained if the solution is heated above 60°C/333 K.)

5 Suction-filter, rinse the crystals with a little cold water and dry between filter papers.

Observations: violet crystals

The formula of chrome alum is:

$$K_2Cr_2(SO_4)_4.24H_2O \quad or$$

$$K_2SO_4.Cr_2(SO_4)_3.24H_2O \quad or$$

$$KCr(SO_4)_2.12H_2O$$

Colours associated with chromium oxidation states

Table 2 shows the colours associated with chromium oxidation states.

Table 2

Oxidation state	Name	Formula	Appearance
+3 state	Chromium(III)	$Cr^{3+}(aq) =$ $[Cr(H_2O)_6]^{3+}(aq)$	Green solution
+3 state	Chromium(III) hydroxide	$Cr(OH)_3(s)$	Green-blue solid
+3 state	Hexahydroxochromate(III)	$[Cr(OH)_6]^{3-}(aq)$	Deep green solution
+6 state	Chromate(VI)	$CrO_4^{2-}(aq)$	Yellow solution
+6 state	Dichromate(VI)	$Cr_2O_7^{2-}(aq)$	Orange solution

Complexes

A **complex** can be positively charged, negatively charged or neutral. Positively and negatively charged complexes are often referred to as **complex ions**.

Complexes are written as $[M(ligand)_x]^{n+ \text{ or } n-}$. The M is the metal atom or ion, for example Cu, Fe, Cr (without any charge if it is the ion). The 'ligand' is the formula of the ligand. x is the number of ligand molecules/ions that are coordinately bonded. $n+$ or $n-$ is the overall charge on the complex. Hexaaqua cations are complexes with six water molecules coordinately bonded to a central metal ion.

A **complex** is a central metal ion or atom surrounded by **ligands** that are coordinately bonded to the central metal atom or ion.

A **ligand** is a neutral molecule or anion with a lone pair of electrons that forms a coordinate bond with a central metal atom or ion in a complex.

Ligands

Neutral molecules:
- aqua is H_2O
- ammine is NH_3
- 1,2-diaminoethane (written 'en') is $H_2NCH_2CH_2NH_2$

Anions:
- chloro is Cl^-
- cyano is CN^-
- SCN^- is thiocyano
- $edta^{4-}$

Monodentate ligands are ligands that use only one lone pair of electrons to form one coordinate bond with the central metal atom or ion in a complex — for example, H_2O, NH_3, Cl^-, CN^-, SCN^-.

Bidentate ligands are ligands that use two lone pairs of electrons to form two coordinate bonds with the central metal atom or ion in a complex — for example, $H_2NCH_2CH_2NH_2$.

Polydentate ligands are ligands that use many lone pairs of electrons to form more than two coordinate bonds with the central metal atom or ion in a complex.

Hexadentate ligands are ligands that use six lone pairs of electrons to form six coordinate bonds with the central metal atom or ion in a complex — for example, $edta^{4-}$.

Charge on the complex and oxidation number

If the ligands in a complex are neutral then the charge on the complex is the same as the oxidation number of the metal atom or ion. For example, in $[Cu(H_2O)_6]^{2+}$ the aqua ligand is neutral and the Cu has an oxidation number of +2.

If the ligands in a complex are negatively charged then the charge on the complex is the oxidation number + (number of ligands × negative charge).

In $[CuCl_4]^{2-}$, the chloro ligand has a charge of −; Cu has an oxidation number of +2 so the complex has a charge of 2−.

The **coordination number** is the number of coordinate bonds formed by the ligands to the central metal atom or ion in a complex. For example:
- $[CuCl_4]^{2-}$ has a coordination number of 4
- $[Ni(NH_3)_6]^{2+}$ has a coordination number of 6
- $[Ni(edta)]^{2-}$ has a coordination number of 6 (as edta is hexadentate)

Shapes of complexes

There are four basic shapes of complexes depending on the coordination number (Table 3).

> **Examiner tip**
> Even though a water molecule contains two lone pairs of electrons, it cannot act as a bidentate ligand as the lone pairs are not far enough separated on the ligand to form separate coordinate bonds. Hexadentate ligands are often referred to as polydentate ligands because they form multiple (more than two) coordinate bonds to the central metal ion.

> **Examiner tip**
> Octahedral complexes containing bidentate ligands form optical isomers due to the two different spatial arrangements of the bidentate ligands around the central metal atom or ion.

Table 3

Coordination number	Shape	Bond angle/°	Examples
2	Linear	180	$[Ag(NH_3)_2]^+$ $[H_3N \rightarrow Ag \leftarrow NH_3]^+$
4	Tetrahedral	109.5	$[CuCl_4]^{2-}$ (structure diagram) $[CoCl_4]^{2-}$ Any other chloro complex
4	Square planar	90	Cisplatin = $[Pt(NH_3)_2Cl_2]$ The structure of cisplatin is discussed on page 37.
6	Octahedral	90	$[Ni(H_2O)_6]^{2+}$ $[Ni(NH_3)_6]^{2+}$ (structure diagram) $[Cr(OH)_6]^{3-}$ $[Cu(NH_3)_4(H_2O)_2]^{2+}$

Examiner tip

The chloro ligand is large so only four Cl^- can fit around the central metal cation, whereas with smaller ligands like water or ammonia six molecules can fit around the central metal cation.

Examiner tip

For the shape of any complex, draw it as you would a linear, a tetrahedral, a square planar or an octahedral complex. You can show the bonds as the coordinate bonds, with the arrows towards the central metal cation/atom.

A **chelating ligand** is one that is polydentate and surrounds the central metal atom or ion, forming multiple coordinate bonds to the central metal atom or ion — for example, edta^{4-}.

Ligand replacement

Some ligands can replace others in a complex. For example, if a solution of edta is added to a solution containing $[Ni(NH_3)_6]^{2+}$, the following ligand replacement reaction occurs:

$$[Ni(NH_3)_6]^{2+}(aq) + edta^{4-}(aq) \rightarrow [Ni(edta)]^{2-}(aq) + 6NH_3(aq)$$

This can be explained in terms of entropy. There are 2 mol of molecules/ions in solution on the left-hand side but 7 mol of molecules/ions in solution on the right-hand side. The right-hand side is more disordered in solution, so there is an increase in entropy, which is favoured.

Use of transition metals and their compounds

There are two forms of platin — cisplatin and transplatin, which are geometric isomers (see Figure 19).

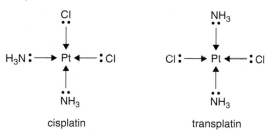

cisplatin   transplatin

Figure 19

The cis- form has two Cl⁻ ligands adjacent to each other and in the trans- form they are opposite each other. Cisplatin has anti-cancer activity.

The molecule has no overall charge as Pt has an oxidation number of +2 and two Cl⁻ ligands are present as well as two neutral NH_3 ligands.

Other uses of transition metals, their compounds and their complexes

Edta can be used to remove hardness from water by forming a complex with dissolved Ca^{2+} and Mg^{2+}, which cause hardness in water.

Edta can also be used to sequester metal ions from blood. For example, Ca^{2+} ions removed from blood can prevent blood clotting. Edta can also remove heavy metal ions such as Hg^+ or Pb^{2+} from blood due to poisoning.

The haemoglobin in our blood is formed from Fe^{2+} ions complexed with a porphyrin ring structure (four nitrogen atoms, each with a lone pair of electrons) and one other coordinate bond from one of four protein chains. The final coordinate bond is from the O_2 molecule, which haemoglobin can carry around the body. The poisonous nature of carbon monoxide (CO) is caused by its ability to form a more stable complex with haemoglobin.

Summary of complexes

Table 4 on page 38 gives a summary of some properties of transition metal complexes.

Examiner tip

Cisplatin works as an anti-cancer drug by cross-linking within a strand of DNA, preventing a cell from replicating its DNA and hence dividing. Uncontrolled cell division is what causes cancer.

Knowledge check 12

State a medical use of cisplatin.

Table 4

Complex	Oxidation number	Coordination number	Shape	Colour
$[Cr(H_2O)_6]^{3+}$	+3	6	Octahedral	Green
$[Mn(H_2O)_6]^{2+}$	+2	6	Octahedral	Pink
$[Fe(H_2O)_6]^{2+}$	+2	6	Octahedral	Green
$[Fe(H_2O)_6]^{3+}$	+3	6	Octahedral	Yellow/orange
$[Co(H_2O)_6]^{2+}$	+2	6	Octahedral	Pink
$[Ni(H_2O)_6]^{2+}$	+2	6	Octahedral	Green
$[Cu(H_2O)_6]^{2+}$	+2	6	Octahedral	Blue
$[Fe(SCN)(H_2O)_5]^{2+}$	+3	6	Octahedral	Blood red
$[Cu(NH_3)_4(H_2O)_2]^{2+}$	+2	6	Octahedral	Deep blue
$[Ni(NH_3)_6]^{2+}$	+2	6	Octahedral	Blue
$[Co(NH_3)_6]^{2+}$	+2	6	Octahedral	Yellow
$[CoCl_4]^{2-}$	+2	4	Tetrahedral	Blue
$[CuCl_4]^{2-}$	+2	4	Tetrahedral	Yellow/green
$[Ni(en)_3]^{2+}$	+2	6	Octahedral	Pink
$[Ni(edta)]^{2-}$	+2	6	Octahedral	Blue
$[V(H_2O)_6]^{2+}$	+2	6	Octahedral	Violet
$[V(H_2O)_6]^{3+}$	+3	6	Octahedral	Green

> **Examiner tip**
> The colour of the precipitate depends on the metal ion present in the solution. Some of the precipitates will redissolve in excess sodium hydroxide solution or excess ammonia solution.

Reactions of hexaaqua cations with sodium hydroxide and aqueous ammonia

Sodium hydroxide solution, NaOH(aq), and ammonia solution, NH_3(aq), contain hydroxide ions, which cause the insoluble precipitate of the metal hydroxide to form when they are added to a solution containing a metal ion.

Table 5 shows some of the hydroxide precipitates with $NaOH(aq)$ and $NH_3(aq)$.

Table 5

Complex	Colour of precipitate	Colour of solution if precipitate redissolves in excess NaOH(aq) and formula of complex formed	Colour of solution if precipitate redissolves in excess NH₃(aq) and formula of complex formed
$[Cr(H_2O)_6]^{3+}$	Green-blue	Deep green solution $[Cr(OH)_6]^{3-}(aq)$	Does not redissolve
$[Mn(H_2O)_6]^{2+}$	White, darkens to brown on standing	Does not redissolve	Does not redissolve
$[Fe(H_2O)_6]^{2+}$	Green	Does not redissolve	Does not redissolve
$[Fe(H_2O)_6]^{3+}$	Brown	Does not redissolve	Does not redissolve
$[Co(H_2O)_6]^{2+}$	Blue	Does not redissolve	Yellow $[Co(NH_3)_6]^{2+}(aq)$
$[Ni(H_2O)_6]^{2+}$	Green	Does not redissolve	Blue $[Ni(NH_3)_6]^{2+}(aq)$
$[Cu(H_2O)_6]^{2+}$	Blue	Does not redissolve	Deep blue $[Cu(NH_3)_4(H_2O)_2]^{2+}(aq)$

Examiner tip

Be sure to state the colour of solutions carefully as described in the introduction. A hyphen (-) between two colours, such as blue-green, means that both colours are required separated by a hyphen.

An insoluble hydroxide such as $Cr(OH)_3$, which redissolves in sodium hydroxide solution, is an amphoteric hydroxide. $Al(OH)_3$ and $Zn(OH)_2$ are other amphoteric hydroxides, which were met in AS Unit 2.

Iron

Iron(III) — when a solution containing Fe^{3+} is mixed with a solution of potassium thiocyanate, a blood red solution is observed (no precipitate):

$$[Fe(H_2O)_6]^{3+} \quad + \quad SCN^- \quad \rightarrow \quad [Fe(H_2O)_5(SCN)]^{2+} \quad + \quad H_2O$$

yellow solution   blood red solution

This is a very sensitive test for Fe^{3+} ions; very small quantities of $Fe^{3+}(aq)$ can be detected.

Vanadium

Vanadium forms the following ions:
- vanadium in the +5 oxidation state: VO_2^+ (also VO_3^-), yellow solution
- vanadium in the +4 oxidation state: VO^{2+}, blue solution
- vanadium in the +3 oxidation state: V^{3+} (can be written as $[V(H_2O)_6]^{3+}$), green solution
- vanadium in the +2 oxidation state: V^{2+} (can be written as: $[V(H_2O)_6]^{2+}$), violet solution

Vanadium can be reduced from +5 to +4 to +3 and finally to +2 using zinc (in the presence of hydrochloric acid). The colour changes are important and so are the equations for the reductions.

Equations for reductions of vanadium

+5 to +4

$$VO_2^+ \quad + \quad 2H^+ \quad + \quad e^- \quad \rightarrow \quad VO^{2+} \quad + \quad H_2O$$

yellow solution ⟶ blue solution

Examiner tip
You can work out these equations, based on oxidation numbers, by revising the Redox section of AS Unit 1. Synoptic questions on oxidation numbers are common at A2.

+4 to +3

$$VO^{2+} \quad + \quad 2H^+ \quad + \quad e^- \quad \rightarrow \quad V^{3+} \quad + \quad H_2O$$

blue solution ⟶ green solution

+3 to +2

$$V^{3+} \quad + \quad e^- \quad \rightarrow \quad V^{2+}$$

green solution ⟶ violet solution

Knowledge check 13
State the colour of vanadium in the +5, +4, +3 and +2 oxidation states.

We will look in more detail at using electrode potentials to predict redox reactions on pages 46–51.

Summary

- Transition metals form compounds of varying oxidation state and varying colour.
- A complex is formed between a transition metal atom or ion and ligands, which are coordinately bonded.
- The coordination number of a complex is the number of coordinate bonds formed from all the ligands to the central metal atom or ion.
- Complexes have linear, tetrahedral, octahedral and square planar shapes.

- Transition metal ions in solution form insoluble hydroxide precipitates when sodium hydroxide **solution** is added or when ammonia **solution** is added.
- The hydroxide precipitates may redissolve when an excess of the sodium hydroxide **solution** or ammonia **solution** is added.
- Ligand replacement reactions may be explained by considering entropy.

A2 inorganic identification tests

Table 6 summarises the analytical tests used to identify ions in inorganic compounds that you are required to know for A2.

Table 6

Test and testing for	How to carry out the test	Typical observations	Deductions from observations *Detail of reactions*
(1) Appearance	Observe colour and state; say whether crystalline or powder	White crystalline solid	Does not contain transition metal ions/not a transition metal compound Compound of group I, group II or an ammonium compound
		Blue crystalline solid	Possibly contains copper(II) ions/Cu^{2+} Copper(II) compound
		Pale green crystalline solid	Possibly contains iron(II) ions/Fe^{2+} Iron(II) compound
		Brown crystalline solid	Possibly contains iron(III) ions/Fe^{3+} Iron(III) compound
		Pink crystalline solid	Possibly contains cobalt(II) ions/Co^{2+} Cobalt(II) compound
		Pale pink crystalline solid	Possibly contains manganese(II) ions/Mn^{2+} Manganese(II) compound
		Green crystalline solid	Possibly contains nickel(II) ions/Ni^{2+} Nickel(II) compound
		Green/violet crystalline solid	Possibly contains chromium(III) ions/Cr^{3+} Chromium(III) compound
		Orange crystalline solid	Possibly contains dichromate(VI) ions/$Cr_2O_7^{2-}$
		Yellow crystalline solid	Possibly contains chromate(VI) ions/CrO_4^{2-}
(2) Solubility in water	Add a few spatula measures of solid to a test tube of deionised water and shake to mix	Dissolves to form a colourless solution	Soluble in water Compound of group I, group II, aluminium, zinc or ammonium
		Dissolves to form a blue solution	Soluble in water Suggests one of: • copper(II) ions/Cu^{2+} ions present • vanadium(IV) ions/VO^{2+} ions present
		Dissolves to form a green solution	Soluble in water Suggests one of: • iron(II) ions/Fe^{2+} ions present • nickel(II) ions/Ni^{2+} ions present • chromium(III) ions/Cr^{3+} ions present • vanadium(III) ions/V^{3+} ions present
		Dissolves to form a (pale) pink solution	Soluble in water Suggests one of: • manganese(II) ions/Mn^{2+} present (pink) • cobalt(II) ions/Co^{2+} present (deeper pink)

Continued

Test and testing for	How to carry out the test	Typical observations	Deductions from observations *Detail of reactions*
		Dissolves to form a yellow solution	Soluble in water Suggests one of: • chromate(VI) ions/CrO_4^{2-} present • vanadium(V) ions present/VO_2^+ present
		Dissolves to form an orange solution	Soluble in water dichromate(VI) ions/$Cr_2O_7^{2-}$ present
		Dissolves to form a yellow/orange solution	Soluble in water iron(III) ions/Fe^{3+} present
		Dissolves to form a violet solution	Soluble in water vanadium(II) ions/V^{2+} ions present
		Does not dissolve	Insoluble in water
(3) Flame test Testing for the presence of metal cations in the compound	Dip a nichrome wire loop in concentrated hydrochloric acid; touch sample with the wire, then hold it in a blue Bunsen flame	Crimson flame	Lithium ion/Li^+ present
		Yellow/orange flame	Sodium ion/Na^+ present
		Lilac (pink through cobalt blue glass)	Potassium ion/K^+ present
		Brick red flame	Calcium ion/Ca^{2+} present
		Green flame	Barium ion/Ba^{2+} present
		Blue-green flame	Copper(II) ion/Cu^{2+} present
(4) Concentrated sulfuric acid Testing for halide ions	Place a spatula measure of solid sample in a test tube and add a few drops of concentrated sulfuric acid	Misty fumes White smoke with glass rod dipped in concentrated ammonia solution	Chloride ion/Cl^- present *Misty fumes are HCl* *White smoke is ammonium chloride, so hydrogen chloride gas released*
		Misty fumes; red-brown vapour	Bromide ion/Br^- present *Misty fumes are HBr* *Red-brown fumes are bromine*
		Misty fumes; violet/purple vapour; smell of rotten eggs; yellow solid; grey-black solid on sides of test tube	Iodide ion/I^- present *Misty fumes are HI* *Violet/purple vapour is iodine* *Smell of rotten eggs is hydrogen sulfide* *Yellow solid is sulfur* *Grey-black solid is iodine*
(5) Silver nitrate solution Testing for halide ions If the background solution is coloured and colour remains, state this colour in the observations	Dissolve a spatula measure of the sample in dilute nitric acid and add a few cm³ of silver nitrate solution Add dilute ammonia solution Add concentrated ammonia solution	White precipitate that redissolves in dilute and concentrated ammonia solution to form a colourless solution	Chloride ion/Cl^- present *White precipitate is AgCl*
		Cream precipitate that does *not* redissolve in dilute ammonia solution but does redissolve in concentrated ammonia to form a colourless solution	Bromide ion/Br^- present *Cream precipitate is AgBr*

Test and testing for	How to carry out the test	Typical observations	Deductions from observations *Detail of reactions*
		Yellow precipitate that does *not* redissolve in either dilute ammonia solution or concentrated ammonia solution	Iodide ions/I^- present *Yellow precipitate is AgI*
		No precipitate	*No halide ions present*
(6) Barium chloride solution Testing for sulfate ions	Dissolve a spatula measure of the sample in dilute nitric acid (or hydrochloric acid) and add a few cm^3 of barium chloride solution	White precipitate	Sulfate ions/SO_4^{2-} present *White precipitate is $BaSO_4$*
		No precipitate formed	*No sulfate ions/ SO_4^{2-} present*
(7) Dilute nitric acid Testing for carbonate and hydrogen carbonate ions The negative part of this test can be the first part of the silver nitrate solution test (test 5) or the barium chloride solution test (test 6)	Place a few cm^3 of dilute nitric acid in a test tube and add a spatula measure of the sample	Effervescence; solid disappears Gas evolved can be passed through limewater in another test tube using a delivery tube — limewater changes from colourless to milky	Carbonate ions/CO_3^{2-} present or hydrogen carbonate ions/HCO_3^- present *Carbon dioxide released from reaction of a carbonate ion or hydrogen carbonate ion with acid*
		No effervescence/no gas produced	*No carbonate ions/CO_3^{2-} or hydrogen carbonate ions/HCO_3^- present*
(8) Magnesium nitrate solution (or magnesium chloride solution) Distinguishing between carbonate and hydrogen carbonate ions	Dissolve a spatula measure of the sample in deionised water and add a few cm^3 of magnesium nitrate solution (or magnesium chloride solution) If no precipitate appears immediately, boil the contents of the test tube	White precipitate appears immediately	Carbonate ions/CO_3^{2-} ions present *White precipitate is magnesium carbonate/ $MgCO_3$*
		Colourless solution — no immediate precipitate White precipitate appears on boiling	Hydrogen carbonate ions/HCO_3^- present *White precipitate on boiling is magnesium carbonate/$MgCO_3$*
		No precipitate even on boiling	*No carbonate ions/CO_3^{2-} or hydrogen carbonate ions/HCO_3^- present*
(9) Potassium thiocyanate (KSCN) solution Testing for iron(III) ions/Fe^{3+} Very sensitive test; detects very small amounts of Fe^{3+}	Dissolve a spatula measure of the sample in deionised water and add a few cm^3 of potassium thiocyanate solution	Blood red solution	Iron(III) ions/Fe^{3+} present *Blood red solution is $[Fe(H_2O)_5SCN]^{2+}$*
		No change	*No iron(III) ions/Fe^{3+} present*

Continued

Test and testing for	How to carry out the test	Typical observations	Deductions from observations *Detail of reactions*
(10) Sodium hydroxide solution Testing for metal cations	Dissolve a spatula measure of the sample in deionised water and add a few drops of sodium hydroxide solution Then add about 5 cm³ of sodium hydroxide solution (adding to excess)	Pale green precipitate that does *not* dissolve in excess sodium hydroxide solution	Iron(II) ions/Fe^{2+} present *Green precipitate is iron(II) hydroxide/$Fe(OH)_2$*
		Brown precipitate that does *not* dissolve in excess sodium hydroxide solution	Iron(III) ions/Fe^{3+} present *Brown precipitate is iron(III) hydroxide/$Fe(OH)_3$*
		White precipitate which does *not* dissolve in excess sodium hydroxide solution	Magnesium ions/Mg^{2+} present *White precipitate is magnesium hydroxide/ $Mg(OH)_2$*
		White precipitate that dissolves in excess sodium hydroxide solution to form a colourless solution	Either aluminium ions/Al^{3+} or zinc ions/Zn^{2+} present *White precipitate is aluminium hydroxide/ $Al(OH)_3$ and colourless solution is $[Al(OH)_4]^-$* or *White precipitate is zinc hydroxide/$Zn(OH)_2$ and colourless solution is $[Zn(OH)_4]^-$*
		Green-blue precipitate that dissolves in excess sodium hydroxide solution to form a green solution	Chromium(III) ions/Cr^{3+} present *Green precipitate is chromium(III) hydroxide/ $Cr(OH)_3$ and green solution is $[Cr(OH)_6]^{3-}$*
		White precipitate that slowly changes to brown on standing and does not dissolve in excess sodium hydroxide solution	Manganese(II) ions/Mn^{2+} present *White precipitate is manganese(II) hydroxide/ $Mn(OH)_2$*
		Blue precipitate that does *not* dissolve in excess sodium hydroxide solution	Either copper(II) ions/Cu^{2+} present (original solution is blue) or cobalt(II) ions/Co^{2+} present (original solution is pink) *Blue precipitate is copper(II) hydroxide/$Cu(OH)_2$ or cobalt(II) hydroxide/$Co(OH)_2$*
		Green precipitate that does *not* dissolve in excess sodium hydroxide solution	Nickel(II) ions/Ni^{2+} present *Green precipitate is nickel(II) hydroxide/$Ni(OH)_2$*
(11) Sodium hydroxide solution Testing for the ammonium ion/ NH_4^+	Place a few cm³ of sodium hydroxide solution in a test tube and add a spatula measure of the sample; warm gently Test any gas evolved using damp red litmus paper or damp universal indicator paper or use a glass rod dipped in concentrated hydrochloric acid	Pungent gas evolved Damp indicator paper changes to blue White smoke with glass rod dipped in concentrated hydrochloric acid	Ammonium ion/NH_4^+ present *Ammonia released from action of alkali (NaOH) on an ammonium compound* *Ammonia gas is alkaline* *White smoke is ammonium chloride from reaction of $NH_3(g)$ with $HCl(g)$ from the concentrated HCl*

Test and testing for	How to carry out the test	Typical observations	Deductions from observations *Detail of reactions*
(12) Aqueous ammonia (dilute ammonia solution) Testing for metal cations	Dissolve a spatula measure of the sample in deionised water and add a few drops of aqueous ammonia Then add about 5 cm^3 of aqueous ammonia (adding until in excess)	White precipitate that does *not* dissolve in excess aqueous ammonia	Either aluminium ions/Al^{3+} or magnesium ions/Mg^{2+} present *White precipitate is either aluminium hydroxide/Al(OH)$_3$ or magnesium hydroxide/Mg(OH)$_2$*
		White precipitate that dissolves in excess aqueous ammonia to form a colourless solution	Zinc ions/Zn^{2+} present *White precipitate is zinc hydroxide/Zn(OH)$_2$*
		White precipitate that slowly darkens to brown on standing and does not dissolve in excess aqueous ammonia	Manganese(II) ions/Mn^{2+} present *White precipitate is manganese(II) hydroxide/Mn(OH)$_2$*
		Green precipitate that does *not* dissolve in excess aqueous ammonia	Iron(II) ions/Fe^{2+} present *Green precipitate is iron(II) hydroxide/Fe(OH)$_2$*
		Brown precipitate that does *not* dissolve in excess aqueous ammonia	Iron(III) ions/Fe^{3+} present *Brown precipitate is iron(III) hydroxide/Fe(OH)$_3$*
		Blue precipitate that dissolves in excess aqueous ammonia to form a yellow solution	Cobalt(II) ions/Co^{2+} present *Blue precipitate is cobalt(II) hydroxide/Co(OH)$_2$ and yellow solution is [Co(NH$_3$)$_6$]$^{2+}$*
		Green precipitate that dissolves in excess aqueous ammonia to form a blue solution	Nickel(II) ions/Ni^{2+} present *Green precipitate is nickel(II) hydroxide/Ni(OH)$_2$ and blue solution is [Ni(NH$_3$)$_6$]$^{2+}$*
		Blue precipitate that dissolves in excess aqueous ammonia to form a deep blue solution	Copper(II) ions/Cu^{2+} present *Blue precipitate is copper(II) hydroxide/Cu(OH)$_2$ and deep blue solution is [Cu(NH$_3$)$_4$(H$_2$O)$_2$]$^{2+}$*
(13) Potassium chromate(VI) solution Testing for barium ions/Ba^{2+}	Dissolve a spatula measure of the sample in deionised water and add a few cm^3 of potassium chromate(VI) solution	Yellow precipitate that redissolves in dilute hydrochloric acid to form a yellow solution	Barium ions/Ba^{2+} present *Yellow precipitate is barium chromate(VI)/BaCrO$_4$*
		No precipitate formed	No barium ions/Ba^{2+} present
(14) Edta solution Testing for nickel(II)/Ni^{2+} ions	Dissolve a spatula measure of the sample in deionised water and add a few cm^3 of edta solution	Green solution changes to blue	Nickel(II) ions/Ni^{2+} present *Green solution is [Ni(H$_2$O)$_6$]$^{2+}$ and blue solution is [Ni(edta)]$^{2-}$*
(15) 1,2-diaminoethane (en) solution Testing for nickel(II)/Ni^{2+} ions	Dissolve a spatula measure of the sample in deionised water and add a few cm^3 of 1,2-diaminoethane (en) solution	Green solution changes to pink	Nickel(II) ions/Ni^{2+} present *Green solution is [Ni(H$_2$O)$_6$]$^{2+}$ and pink solution is [Ni(en)$_3$]$^{2+}$*

Continued

Test and testing for	How to carry out the test	Typical observations	Deductions from observations *Detail of reactions*
(16) Heating a sample of the solid	Place a spatula measure of the sample in a test tube and heat gently	Colourless liquid forms on upper walls of test tube Change in solid appearance of crystals and possible change in colour	Water of crystallisation present Hydrated salt

Examiner tip

When describing tests for ions, you must be able to give full practical details of how to carry out the tests. Make sure you include the word solution — for example, 'To a solution of the substance, add ammonia solution'. Leaving out the term 'solution' would cost you marks. Remember, also, that a negative result can be as useful as a positive result.

Electrode potentials

When a metal is placed in a solution of its ions, an equilibrium is established between the ions in the solution and the metal atoms.

The equilibrium can be represented by a half-equation:

$$M^{n+}(aq) + ne^- \rightleftharpoons M(s)$$

For example:

$$Zn^{2+}(aq) + 2e^- \rightleftharpoons Zn(s)$$

$$Fe^{2+}(aq) + 2e^- \rightleftharpoons Fe(s)$$

The ions are aqueous and the metal is solid.
- The half-equations are written as reduction reactions (gain of electrons).
- The metal dipping into a solution of its ions is called a half-cell.
- Two half-cells combined are called a cell.
- In one of the half-cells an oxidation must occur and in the other a reduction must occur.
- In any electrochemical reaction, there must be a reduction and an oxidation.

Standard electrode potentials

The **standard electrode potential** is the potential difference measured when a half-cell is connected to the standard hydrogen electrode under standard conditions.

The electrode potential is a relative measure of the feasibility of the reduction occurring. Electrode potentials are represented by $E^\ominus$ and are measured in volts (V). The electrode potential must be stated with a sign and the units V. For example:

$$Fe^{2+} + 2e^- \rightleftharpoons Fe \qquad\qquad E^\ominus = -0.44\,V$$

$$Zn^{2+} + 2e^- \rightleftharpoons Zn \qquad\qquad E^\ominus = -0.76\,V$$

$$I_2 + 2e^- \rightleftharpoons 2I^- \qquad\qquad E^\ominus = +0.54\,V$$

A negative electrode potential indicates that the reduction reaction is not feasible unless a more feasible oxidation takes place.

The reduction of iron(II) ions to iron is not feasible but if iron(II) ions were mixed with zinc metal, the zinc metal would oxidise:

$$Zn(s) \rightarrow Zn^{2+}(aq) + 2e^- \qquad +0.76\,V$$

and the iron(II) would be reduced to iron

$$Fe^{2+}(aq) + 2e^- \rightarrow Fe(s) \qquad -0.44\,V$$

Electromotive force (emf)

The **electromotive force (emf)** of a complete cell is the total value of the oxidation and reduction standard electrode potentials when the two half-cells are combined.

- A positive emf indicates a feasible reaction.
- A negative emf indicates an unfeasible reaction.
- The emf always relates to the overall redox reaction (oxidation and reduction combined).

The overall electromotive force (emf) of the above cell is +0.76 – 0.44 = +0.32 V, so this overall reaction is feasible.

The $E^\ominus$ values given are standard electrode potentials. 'Standard' means they have been compared to the standard hydrogen electrode.

Features of the standard hydrogen electrode

Figure 20 shows the general features of the standard hydrogen electrode.

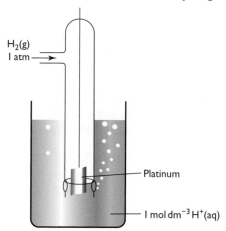

$H_2(g)$
1 atm

Platinum

1 mol dm^{-3} H$^+$(aq)

Figure 20 The standard hydrogen electrode

The required conditions are:
- platinum electrode
- 1 mol dm^{-3} hydrogen ions in solution
- H_2 gas at 1 atm pressure
- temperature should be 25°C

The standard electrode potential of a standard hydrogen electrode is 0.00 V.

Examiner tip
Standard electrode potentials are not measured per mole of anything as they are all carried out under standard solution conditions. It does not matter how many moles of each reactant react.

The **electromotive force (emf)** is the potential difference measured when two half-cells are connected.

Knowledge check 14
What conditions are required for the standard hydrogen electrode?

Combination of half-cells

Two half-cells can be combined using a salt bridge and an external circuit containing a high-resistance voltmeter to produce a cell (Figure 21). The salt bridge is usually filter paper soaked in potassium nitrate solution, which dips into both half-cell solutions. The salt bridge allows electrical connection between the half-cells without allowing them to mix.

- The left-hand half-cell (by convention) is the one in which oxidation occurs.
- The right-hand half-cell (by convention) is the one in which reduction occurs.

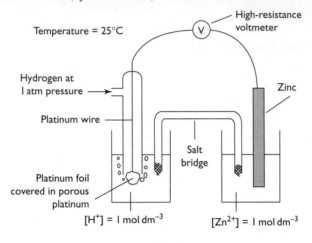

Figure 21 Two half-cells combined

Cell notation

Examiner tip

State symbols are often included in cell notation: ions are in solution, so (aq) is used; metals are solid, so (s) is used; and gases are represented by (g). The use of right-hand side minus left-hand side changes the value of the reduction on the left-hand side into an oxidation by reversing the sign. This is the same process as simply changing the sign of the oxidation and adding the values.

Cells are written as:

   oxidation at left-hand half cell ‖ reduction at right hand half cell

For example, $Zn|Zn^{2+}||Cu^{2+}|Cu$, where:
- ‖ represents the salt bridge
- $Zn|Zn^{2+}$ represents the oxidation reaction $Zn \rightarrow Zn^{2+} + 2e^-$
- $Cu^{2+}|Cu$ represents the reduction reaction $Cu^{2+} + 2e^- \rightarrow Cu$

The overall emf of the cell $= E_{rhs}^{\ominus} - E_{lhs}^{\ominus}$ (right hand side − left hand side).
- For $Zn^{2+} + 2e^- \rightarrow Zn$ $E^{\ominus} = -0.76\,V$
- For $Cu^{2+} + 2e^- \rightarrow Cu$ $E^{\ominus} = +0.34\,V$

Therefore, for the cell $Zn|Zn^{2+}||Cu^{2+}|Cu$:

   emf $= +0.34 - (-0.76) = +1.10\,V$

This reaction is feasible as the overall emf is positive.

CCEA A2 Chemistry

Reactivity series

Take the following standard electrode potentials:

$$Zn^{2+} + 2e^- \rightarrow Zn \qquad E^\ominus = -0.76\,V$$

$$Cu^{2+} + 2e^- \rightarrow Cu \qquad E^\ominus = +0.34\,V$$

$$Mg^{2+} + 2e^- \rightarrow Mg \qquad E^\ominus = -2.37\,V$$

$$Fe^{2+} + 2e^- \rightarrow Fe \qquad E^\ominus = -0.44\,V$$

The electrode potential for the reverse oxidation reaction gives a measure of the reactivity of the metal since the most reactive metal will form ions most easily.

From these values, it is clear that it is most feasible for Mg to form its ions (+2.37 V), followed by Zn (+0.76 V), followed by Fe (+0.44 V) and least of all Cu (−0.34 V). This explains the reactivity of magnesium and copper's lack of reactivity.

Redox potentials applied to vanadium chemistry

Vanadium oxidation state change	Half equation	$E^\ominus$/V
+5 to +4	$VO_2^+ + 2H^+ + e^- \rightarrow VO^{2+} + H_2O$	+1.00
+4 to +3	$VO^{2+} + 2H^+ + e^- \rightarrow V^{3+} + H_2O$	+0.32
+3 to +2	$V^{3+} + e^- \rightarrow V^{2+}$	−0.26

Worked example

Which reducing agent will reduce vanadium from the +5 oxidation state to the +3 oxidation state?

    A   iodine

    B   iron

    C   sulfur dioxide

    D   zinc

given the following standard redox potentials:

			$E^\ominus$/V
$Zn^{2+}(aq) + 2e^-$	$\rightleftharpoons$	$Zn(s)$	−0.76
$Fe^{2+}(aq) + 2e^-$	$\rightleftharpoons$	$Fe(s)$	−0.44
$SO_4^{2-}(aq) + 4H^+(aq) + 2e^-$	$\rightleftharpoons$	$2H_2O(l) + SO_2(g)$	+0.17
$I_2(aq) + 2e^-$	$\rightleftharpoons$	$2I^-(aq)$	+0.54

The choice has to be from the right of these half-equations because a substance that is to be oxidised (i.e. lose electrons) must be chosen. Any substance that is on the left of one of these equations (for example iodine) can be ruled out because it would be reduced.

Each reaction is taken in turn, with each stage of the reduction of vanadium. Try the oxidation of Fe to Fe^{2+}, which has a potential of +0.44 V:

$$VO_2^+ + 2H^+ + e^- \rightarrow VO^{2+} + H_2O \qquad +1.00\,V$$

$$Fe \rightarrow Fe^{2+} + 2e^- \qquad +0.44\,V$$

$$emf = +1.44\,V\ feasible$$

$$VO^{2+} + 2H^+ + e^- \rightarrow V^{3+} + H_2O \qquad +0.32\,V$$

$$Fe \rightarrow Fe^{2+} + 2e^- \qquad +0.44\,V$$

$$emf = +0.76\,V\ feasible$$

$$V^{3+} + e^- \rightarrow V^{2+} \qquad -0.26\,V$$

$$Fe \rightarrow Fe^{2+} + 2e^- \qquad +0.44\,V$$

$$emf = +0.18\,V\ feasible$$

Fe cannot be the answer because Fe will reduce vanadium from +5 to +2.

Try the oxidation of sulfur dioxide to sulfate:

$$VO_2^+ + 2H^+ + e^- \rightarrow VO^{2+} + H_2O \qquad +1.00\,V$$

$$2H_2O(l) + SO_2(g) \rightarrow SO_4^{2-}(aq) + 4H^+(aq) + 2e^- \qquad -0.17\,V$$

$$emf = +0.83\,V\ feasible$$

$$VO^{2+} + 2H^+ + e^- \rightarrow V^{3+} + H_2O \qquad +0.32\,V$$

$$2H_2O(l) + SO_2(g) \rightarrow SO_4^{2-}(aq) + 4H^+(aq) + 2e^- \qquad -0.17\,V$$

$$emf = +0.15\,V\ feasible$$

$$V^{3+} + e^- \rightarrow V^{2+} \qquad -0.26\,V$$

$$2H_2O(l) + SO_2(g) \rightarrow SO_4^{2-}(aq) + 4H^+(aq) + 2e^- \qquad -0.17\,V$$

$$emf = -0.43\,V\ not\ feasible$$

Sulfur dioxide (SO_2) is the answer because it will reduce vanadium from +5 to +3 but will not reduce vanadium from +3 to +2. Zinc will reduce vanadium from +5 to +2 and iodide ions (which were not given in the question) will reduce vanadium from +5 to +4, but no further.

Oxidising agents and reducing agents

Oxidising agents are easily reduced and reducing agents are easily oxidised.

$$E^\ominus / V$$

$Zn^{2+}(aq) + 2e^-$	$\rightleftharpoons$	$Zn(s)$	-0.76
$Fe^{2+}(aq) + 2e^-$	$\rightleftharpoons$	$Fe(s)$	-0.44
$SO_4^{2-}(aq) + 4H^+(aq) + 2e^-$	$\rightleftharpoons$	$2H_2O(l) + SO_2(g)$	$+0.17$
$I_2(aq) + 2e^-$	$\rightleftharpoons$	$2I^-(aq)$	$+0.54$

The best reducing agent in the above set of half equations is zinc because it is most easily oxidised ($Zn \rightarrow Zn^{2+} + 2e^-$ is $+0.76\,V$). The best oxidising agent is iodine ($I_2 + 2e^- \rightarrow 2I^-$ is $+0.54\,V$).

Summary

- Standard electrode potentials give a measure in volts (V) of the feasibility of a half-cell reaction.
- The emf (electromotive force) is the combination of the standard electrode potentials for the two half-cell reactions.
- A positive emf indicates a feasible reaction whereas a negative emf indicates a reaction that is not feasible.
- The standard hydrogen electrode is measured with 1 atm pressure of H_2, $1\,mol\,dm^{-3}$ of H^+ ions and at 25°C (298 K).
- The strongest reducing agent (reductant) is the one that is most easily oxidised.
- The strongest oxidising agent (oxidant) is the one that is most easily reduced.

Arenes

Benzene

A molecule of benzene, C_6H_6, consists of six carbon atoms in a hexagonal planar ring arrangement. Each carbon atom is bonded covalently to two other carbon atoms in the ring and a hydrogen atom. Each carbon atom has a *p* electron that is not bonded. The *p* orbitals containing these electrons can overlap to form a π-delocalised system of electrons above and below the plane of the main ring. When it was discovered and analysed, it was thought that benzene contained three single C—C bonds and three double C=C bonds. This structure is called the Kekulé structure of benzene and is drawn as shown in Figure 22.

Figure 22 The Kekulé structure of benzene

However, the following evidence has shown that the model with the delocalised system of electrons is the most appropriate:

- The carbon–carbon bonds in benzene were all shown to be the same length and intermediate in length between a C—C bond and a C=C bond. This would not be consistent with three C—C bonds and three C=C bonds.

- The energy required to hydrogenate 1 mol of benzene (i.e. to react the three $C\!=\!C$ bonds with H_2) should be three times the energy required to hydrogenate 1 mol of cyclohexene (C_6H_{10}) to cyclohexane (C_6H_{12}) if the Kekulé structure is correct. This would mean that when 1 mol of benzene undergoes complete hydrogenation, the energy change should be $-360\,kJ\,mol^{-1}$. However, the energy change is actually $-208\,kJ\,mol^{-1}$ (see Figure 23). This extra energy (152 kJ) is the stability that is conferred by the π-delocalised system of electrons.

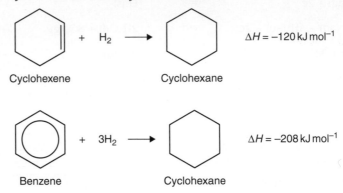

Figure 23 Evidence for a π-delocalised system of electrons in benzene

Figure 24 shows the formation of the delocalised system structure of benzene.

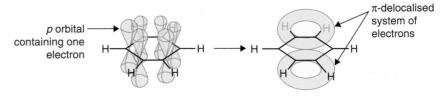

Figure 24 The delocalised system structure of benzene

The structure of benzene is shown in Figure 25. This structure shows the π-delocalised system of electrons.

Figure 25 Benzene

Examiner tip
The hydrogen atoms bonded to the carbon atoms in benzene are not shown but they are present. Don't forget about them when working out the formula of a benzene compound. This is particularly important when working out the RMM of a benzene compound.

- Benzene is obtained from petroleum (crude oil).
- Benzene is a colourless liquid at room temperature and pressure.
- The delocalised structure is used in all structures containing a benzene ring.
- Each point on the hexagon represents one carbon atom with one hydrogen atom bonded to the carbon atom.

CCEA A2 Chemistry

- The circle represents the delocalised π cloud of electrons. There are six electrons in the π-delocalised system. The main bonds between the carbon atoms and between carbon and hydrogen atoms in benzene are σ bonds; each carbon atom forms three σ bonds. The fourth electrons in a *p* orbital at each carbon atom are delocalised around the system to form a π-delocalised system of electrons.
- Benzene does not undergo addition reactions easily owing to the stability of the π-delocalised system of electrons.
- Benzene does not react readily with bromine, whereas alkenes do react with bromine.
- Benzene undergoes **electrophilic substitution reactions**.

> **Delocalisation** means that the π electrons are spread over several atoms.

> An **electrophile** is an electron-deficient species or a species with a positive charge that attacks an electron-rich region and accepts a pair of electrons.

> A **substitution reaction** is a reaction where one atom or group is replaced by another group or atom.

Substituted benzene compounds

There are many substituted benzene compounds. It is important to be able to recognise them and write their formulae. Remember that each group substituted onto the benzene ring means one less hydrogen atom. Tables 7–9 show the formulae of some substituted benzene compounds that you will meet in A2 chemistry.

Table 7

Compound	Phenol	Methylbenzene (toluene)	Phenylamine (aniline)
Formula	C_6H_5OH	$C_6H_5CH_3$	$C_6H_5NH_2$
Structural formula	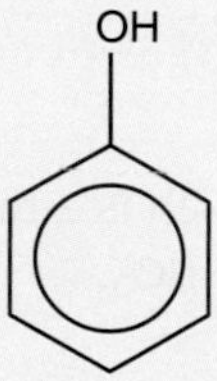	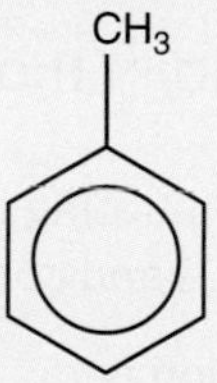	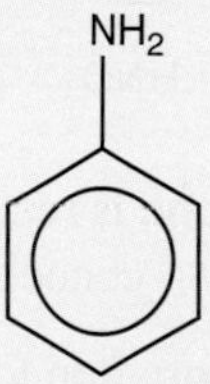

Table 8

Compound	Iodobenzene	Bromobenzene	Benzoic acid
Formula	C_6H_5I	C_6H_5Br	C_6H_5COOH
Structural formula	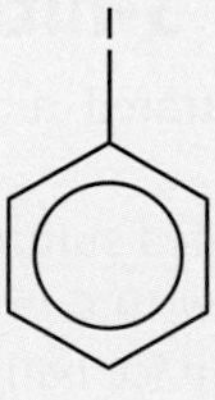	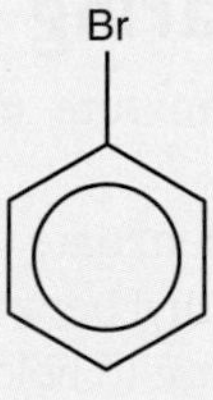	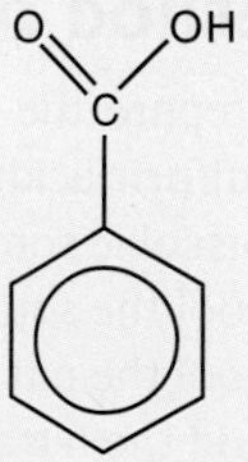

Table 9

Compound	Methyl benzoate	Methyl 3-nitrobenzoate	Benzene diazonium chloride
Formula	$CH_3OOCC_6H_5$	$CH_3OOCC_6H_4NO_2$	$C_6H_5N_2Cl$
Structural formula			

Reactions of benzene

Nitration

Benzene can be nitrated (have an H atom substituted for an NO_2 group). The mechanism of nitration is **electrophilic substitution**. The electrophile is the nitronium ion (or nitryl cation), which is NO_2^+.

The nitronium ion is formed from the reaction between concentrated sulfuric acid and concentrated nitric acid:

$$HNO_3 + 2H_2SO_4 \rightarrow NO_2^+ + H_3O^+ + 2HSO_4^-$$

Benzene is reacted with a nitrating mixture, which is a mixture of two concentrated acids — concentrated H_2SO_4 and concentrated HNO_3.

The equation for the nitration is:

$$C_6H_6 + NO_2^+ \rightarrow C_6H_5NO_2 + H^+$$

or

$$C_6H_6 + HNO_3 \rightarrow C_6H_5NO_2 + H_2O$$

The product is nitrobenzene, $C_6H_5NO_2$.

Method of preparing methyl 3-nitrobenzoate

1 Prepare the nitrating mixture (mix concentrated nitric acid and concentrated sulfuric acid).
2 Dissolve some methyl benzoate in concentrated sulfuric acid.
3 Cool the solution of methyl benzoate to below 10°C in an ice bath.
4 Cool the nitrating mixture to below 10°C in an ice bath.
5 Add the nitrating mixture to methyl benzoate slowly/dropwise.
6 Maintain the temperature below 10°C.

The mixture is kept below 10°C to prevent multiple nitrations of benzene. Multiple nitrations would lead to the formation of an explosive compound.

7 Stand at room temperature for 10 minutes.

8 Pour the mixture onto crushed ice to form the crystals.

9 Suction-filter off the solid methyl 3-nitrobenzoate (see Figure 26). Wash the crystals.

Suction filtration is used because it is faster and gives a drier product.

10 Dissolve the solid in a minimum volume of hot ethanol.

11 Filter (through fluted filter paper) while hot.

The fluted filter paper minimises contact with the cold funnel, which would cause crystallisation. Suction filtration can never be used at this stage because the cold air being drawn through would cool the solution and crystallisation would occur on the filter paper.

12 Allow to cool and crystallise.

13 Suction-filter and wash crystals with a little ice-cold solvent.

Methyl 3-nitrobenzoate is obtained as a **cream solid**.

Mechanism of nitration

Figure 27 shows how the electrophilic substitution mechanism for the nitration of methyl benzoate occurs.

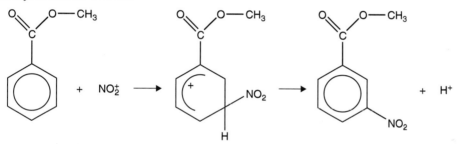

Figure 27 Electrophilic substitution mechanism for the nitration of methyl benzoate

Monohalogenation

The main monohalogenation of benzene that is studied is the monobromination of benzene using bromine in the presence of iron or iron(III) bromide (Figure 28a). Bromine reacts with benzene only in the presence of Fe or $FeBr_3$ (the Fe is converted to $FeBr_3$ by the reaction: $2Fe + 3Br_2 \rightarrow 2FeBr_3$).

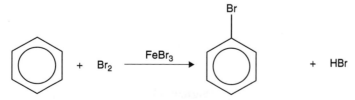

Figure 28a Monobromination of benzene

The mechanism for the bromination of benzene is given in Figure 28b. In the first stage the Br_2 becomes polarised as it approaches the benzene ring. The $FeBr_3$ acts as a halogen carrier holding the Br^-, while the other bromine atom accepts a pair of

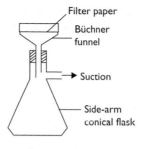

Figure 26 Suction filtration apparatus

Filter paper
Büchner funnel
Suction
Side-arm conical flask

> **Examiner tip**
> Ethanol is a good choice for solvent, but use the solvent named in the method if one is given in a practical exam scenario. The solid being prepared should be soluble in the hot solvent and have a low solubility in the cold solvent. A minimum volume of hot solvent is used to ensure that as much of the product is obtained as possible.

> **Examiner tip**
> Stages 9 to 13 in the method are standard for purifying an organic solid and this process is called **recrystallisation**. You should be familiar with the processes from AS Unit 2 and should be able to draw a diagram of suction filtration and explain why it is used. Often the whole recrystallisation process is described. The purity of the sample can be checked by carrying out a melting-point determination. A pure sample has a sharp melting point. An impure sample melts over a range and at a lower value than expected.

> **Examiner tip**
> Compare the reaction of ethene with bromine, which happens spontaneously and is an addition reaction, with the reaction of benzene with bromine, which requires iron (or iron(III) bromide) and is a substitution reaction — this is due to the stability of the delocalised system of electrons.

Examiner tip

For any other electrophilic substitution reaction of benzene, the mechanism is similar. The electrophile will have a $\delta+$ (as with the polarised bromine molecule) or often even a positive charge (such as NO_2^+). It is possible to show the bromination of benzene using Br^+ as the electrophile and even $CH_3CH_2^+$ can be shown to react with benzene to form ethylbenzene ($C_6H_5CH_2CH_3$).

Knowledge check 16

Name the mechanism by which benzene reacts with bromine.

Examiner tip

Questions are often asked about the number of isomers of substituted benzene compounds — for example, the number of isomers that have formula $C_6H_4Br_2$. The answer is three because you can have 1,2-dibromobenzene, 1,3-dibromobenzene and 1,4-dibromobenzene. 1,5-dibromobenzene does not exist because it is the same as 1,3-dibromobenzene. 2,3-dibromobenzene does not exist because it is the same as 1,2-dibromobenzene. Draw them to make sure you understand.

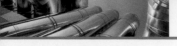

electrons from the delocalised cloud of electrons in the benzene ring. The electrons in the C–H bond go back into the ring to reform the delocalised cloud. Finally the $FeBr_4^-$ reacts with the H^+ to regenerate the $FeBr_3$ and form HBr.

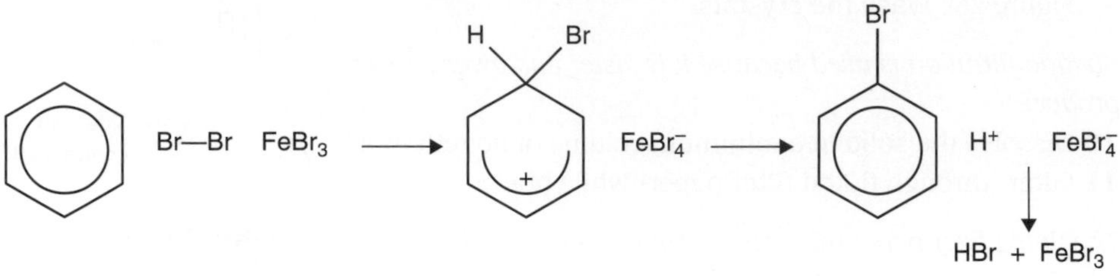

Figure 28b Mechanism for bromination of benzene

Multiple substituted benzene compounds

The carbon atoms in the benzene ring are numbered from 1 to 6. The highest priority group that is bonded to the ring is given position 1 and the position of the other groups bonded to the ring indicated using numbers.

Worked example 1

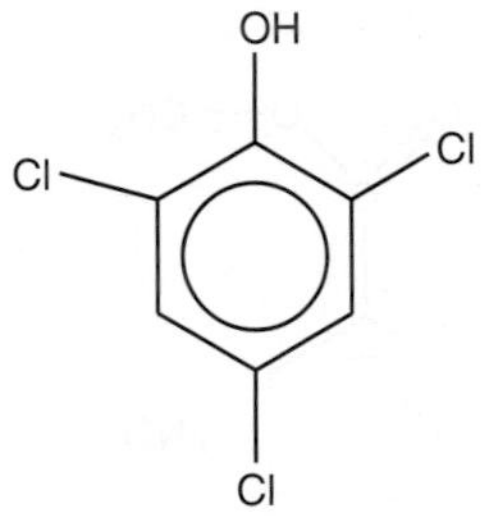

Figure 29

The compound shown in Figure 29 is called 2,4,6-trichlorophenol. The OH group makes the main name for the molecule phenol (the OH group is then considered to be position 1 in the ring) and the three Cl atoms are labelled with positions 2, 4 and 6.

Worked example 2

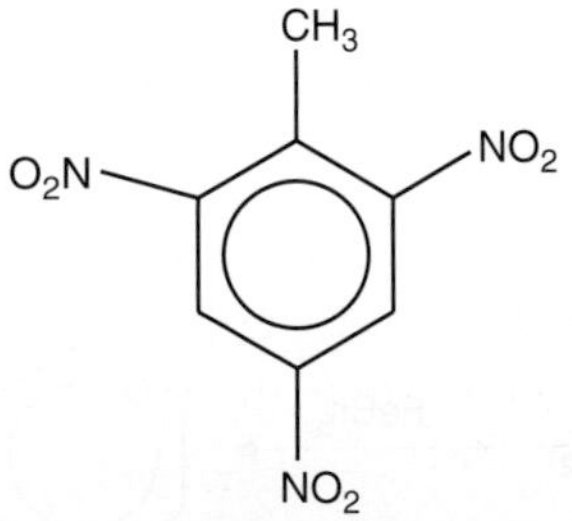

Figure 30

The compound shown in Figure 30 is called 2-methyl-1,3,5-trinitrobenzene. The nitro (NO_2) groups have higher priority than the methyl (CH_3) group so the nitro groups are labelled as positions 1, 3 and 5. The groups are named alphabetically so methyl comes before nitro as both are substituent groups.

Fused benzene ring structures

There are several different fused ring structures of benzene, such as the two shown in Figure 31.

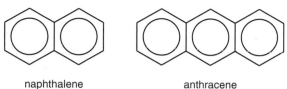

naphthalene   anthracene

Figure 31 Two fused ring structures of benzene

The molecular formula of naphthalene is $C_{10}H_8$. There are ten carbon atoms and eight hydrogen atoms in one molecule because the carbon atoms at the intersection of the rings do not have hydrogen atoms bonded to them. The molecular formula for anthracene is $C_{14}H_{10}$.

Reactivity of benzene compared with that of an alkene (usually ethene)

Benzene undergoes electrophilic substitution reactions. Alkenes (ethene) undergo electrophilic addition reactions where the π bond is broken. Benzene undergoes substitution reactions because of the stability of the π-delocalised system of electrons. The π covalent bond in alkenes is more open to electrophilic addition reactions than the π-delocalised system of electrons in benzene.

- Benzene compounds are stable due to the π-delocalised system of electrons.
- Benzene is C_6H_6 and is a planar hexagonal ring structure consisting of six delocalised electrons.
- Benzene compounds undergo electrophilic substitution reactions.
- Methyl 3-nitrobenzoate can be prepared by nitration of methyl benzoate.

Summary

Amines

An amine is a nitrogen-containing organic compound. Where R is an alkyl or aromatic group:
- a **primary (1°) amine** has the structure $R-NH_2$
- a **secondary (2°) amine** has the structure R_2NH
- a **tertiary (3°) amine** has the structure R_3N

Table 10 shows the formulae and classification of some common examples of amines.

Examiner tip
The more fused rings that are present in a molecule, the greater the degree of π-delocalisation. The energy levels in the molecule become closer together and the absorbance moves towards the visible region of the electromagnetic spectrum (from the ultraviolet region). Pentacene ($C_{22}H_{14}$) contains five fused benzene rings and is red in colour because it absorbs in the visible region and the complementary colour observed is red. Benzene, naphthalene and anthracene are colourless because they absorb in the ultraviolet region of the electromagnetic spectrum.

A **primary amine** has one carbon atom bonded directly to the N atom and therefore has the $-NH_2$ group.

A **secondary amine** has two carbon atoms bonded directly to the N atom:

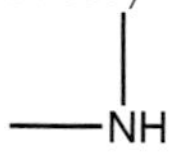

A **tertiary amine** has three carbon atoms bonded directly to the N atom:

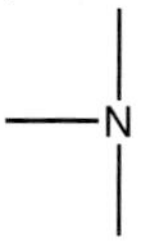

Table 10

Name	Formula	Structural formula	Classification
Methylamine	CH_3NH_2		Primary
Ethylamine	$CH_3CH_2NH_2$		Primary
Dimethylamine	$(CH_3)_2NH$		Secondary
Trimethylamine	$(CH_3)_3N$		Tertiary
Phenylamine (aniline)	$C_6H_5NH_2$		Primary

Aromatic amines have chemical and physical properties that are different from aliphatic amines.

Methylamine and ethylamine are gases; propylamine and butylamine are liquids.

The N–H bond is polar (the N is δ– and the H is δ+). Hydrogen bonds form between amine molecules. This gives them higher melting and boiling points than similar RMM alkanes. Hydrogen bonds form between short-chain amine molecules and water. This makes short-chain amines soluble in water.

Preparation of aliphatic amines from other organic compounds

Reduction of nitriles

Nitriles contain the $-C\equiv N$ functional group. Nitriles can be reduced to primary amines using lithal ($LiAlH_4$). The nitrile is refluxed with lithal in dry ether. [H] can be used to represent the reducing agent. For example:

$$CH_3C{\equiv}N \quad + \quad 4[H] \quad \rightarrow \quad CH_3CH_2NH_2$$

ethanenitrile   reducing agent   ethylamine

Reaction of halogenoalkanes with ammonia

Halogenoalkanes are mixed with ammonia in ethanolic solution and heated in a sealed tube in the absence of air. The tube is opened in sodium hydroxide solution, which converts the alkylammonium ion to the amine. For example:

$$CH_3CH_2Br \quad + \quad NH_3 \quad \rightarrow \quad CH_3CH_2NH_2 \quad + \quad HBr$$

bromoethane   ammonia   ethylamine   hydrogen bromide

Preparation of phenylamine from nitrobenzene

This is the only reduction on the A-level course that does not use lithal as the standard reducing agent. The reducing agent used is tin and concentrated hydrochloric acid. Again [H] can be used to represent the reducing agent.

$$C_6H_5NO_2 \quad + \quad 6[H] \quad \rightarrow \quad C_6H_5NH_2 \quad + \quad 2H_2O$$

nitrobenzene   reducing agent   phenylamine   water

The process involves refluxing the nitrobenzene with tin and concentrated hydrochloric acid, followed by addition of concentrated sodium hydroxide solution for the liberation of the free amine. The amine is not formed when hydrochloric acid is present; instead, phenylammonium chloride is formed — $C_6H_5NH_3Cl$. The sodium hydroxide converts the phenylammonium chloride to phenylamine:

$$C_6H_5NH_3Cl \quad + \quad NaOH \quad \rightarrow \quad C_6H_5NH_2 \quad + \quad NaCl \quad + \quad H_2O$$

phenylammonium   sodium   phenylamine
chloride   hydroxide

Chemical properties of aliphatic and aromatic amines

Amines as bases

All amines act as bases and so they accept a proton (H^+) from an acid. Amines can do this because the N atom has a lone pair of electrons that can form a coordinate bond with an H^+ ion. The positive ion formed is called an alkylammonium ion or a phenylammonium ion. For example:

$$CH_3NH_2 \quad + \quad HCl \quad \rightarrow \quad CH_3NH_3Cl$$

methylamine   hydrochloric acid   methylammonium chloride

> **Examiner tip**
> You should revise the use of [H] to represent a reducing agent from AS Unit 2. If oxygen atoms are to be removed from reactant molecules, the equation can be balanced using water on the right-hand side.

> **Examiner tip**
> Amines can be regarded as substituted ammonia molecules. Examine the reaction of ammonia, NH_3, and substitute an H atom for a methyl group and you get CH_3NH_2, which is methylamine; substitute two H atoms for two ethyl groups and you get $(C_2H_5)_2NH$, which is diethylamine.

Methyl ammonium chloride contains the methylammonium ion, $CH_3NH_3^+$, and the chloride ion, Cl^-. For example:

$$2C_6H_5NH_2 \quad + \quad H_2SO_4 \quad \rightarrow \quad (C_6H_5NH_3)_2SO_4$$
$$\text{phenylamine} \qquad \qquad \text{sulfuric acid} \qquad \qquad \text{phenylammonium sulfate}$$

Phenylammonium sulfate contains the phenylammonium ion, $C_6H_5NH_3^+$, and the sulfate ion, SO_4^{2-}. Two phenylammonium ions are required for each sulfate ion because of the charge on the sulfate.

Amines in aqueous solution are alkaline because of their reaction with water. For example:

$$CH_3NH_2 \quad + \quad H_2O \quad \rightleftharpoons \quad CH_3NH_3^+ \quad + \quad OH^-$$
$$\text{methylamine} \qquad \text{water} \qquad \text{methylammonium ion} \qquad \text{hydroxide ion}$$

Basicity of amines

The ability to accept the H^+ ion depends on the groups attached to the N atom.

A benzene ring (i.e. phenylamine) withdraws electrons from the C–N bond. This stabilises the lone pair on the N atom, which makes phenylamine a weaker base than ammonia.

An alkyl group is electron donating. This pushes electrons further towards the N atom, which destabilises the lone pair on the N atom and makes an alkylamine a stronger base than ammonia.

Order of basicity

The order of basicity decreases from primary amines to ammonia to phenylamine. An aqueous solution of the base would be most alkaline (highest pH) for a primary amine, less alkaline for ammonia and least alkaline (lowest pH) for phenylamine.

primary amine	ammonia	phenylamine

decreasing basicity →

Reaction of amines with ethanoyl chloride

Amines can form a substituted amide with ethanoyl chloride. An example is shown in Figure 32.

$$CH_3CH_2NH_2 \quad + \quad CH_3COCl \quad \rightarrow \quad CH_3CONHCH_2CH_3 \quad + \quad HCl$$

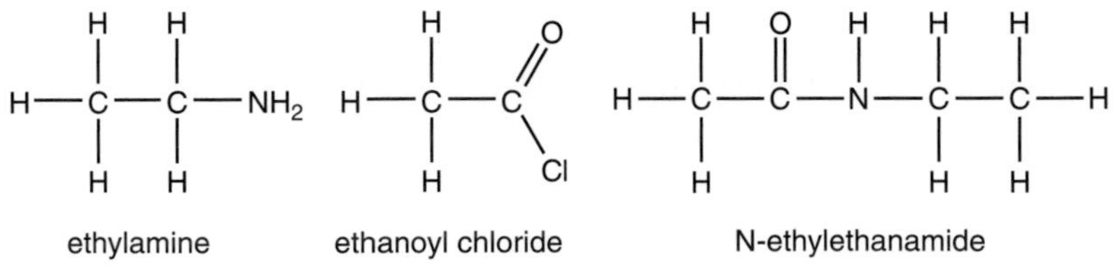

ethylamine   ethanoyl chloride   N-ethylethanamide

Figure 32

Reaction with nitrous acid, HNO_2

Nitrous acid is prepared in situ (in the reaction vessel) from sodium nitrite and hydrochloric acid:

$$NaNO_2 + HCl \rightarrow HNO_2 + NaCl$$

Amines react with nitrous acid differently depending on whether the amine is aliphatic or aromatic and on the temperature of the reaction mixture.

Aromatic

Below 5°C phenylamine reacts with nitrous acid to form the benzene diazonium ion, $C_6H_5N_2^+$ (Figure 33).

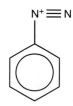

Figure 33 The benzene diazonium ion

Phenylamine, $C_6H_5NH_2$, is reacted with nitrous acid in situ below 5°C. The diazonium ion is only stable below 5°C. Because of the presence of HCl in the reaction mixture, benzene diazonium chloride is the salt usually formed.

Reactions of the benzene diazonium ion

On warming

Benzene diazonium chloride is unstable when warmed. It reacts with water in the aqueous solution to form phenol:

$$C_6H_5N_2Cl \quad + \quad H_2O \quad \rightarrow \quad C_6H_5OH \quad + \quad N_2 \quad + \quad HCl$$

benzene diazonium   phenol
chloride

Or the equation can be written directly from phenylamine:

$$C_6H_5NH_2 \quad + \quad HNO_2 \quad \rightarrow \quad C_6H_5OH \quad + \quad N_2 \quad + \quad H_2O$$

phenylamine   phenol

Bubbles of a colourless gas are produced in this reaction — this is nitrogen, N_2.

Examiner tip

If you are asked to draw the benzene diazonium ion, make sure the + charge is placed on the nitrogen atom with four covalent bonds. There must be three bonds between the N atoms.

Knowledge check 18

Write an equation for the in-situ formation of nitrous acid from sodium nitrite and hydrochloric acid.

With potassium iodide solution

Benzene diazonium chloride reacts with potassium iodide solution when warmed. It forms iodobenzene and releases a colourless gas (again, this gas is nitrogen, N_2):

$$C_6H_5N_2Cl \quad + \quad KI \quad \rightarrow \quad C_6H_5I \quad + \quad N_2 \quad + \quad KCl$$

benzene diazonium   iodobenzene
chloride

With phenol

A **coupling reaction** is one in which two aromatic compounds (benzene rings) are linked through an azo group (—N=N—).

Benzene diazonium chloride reacts with phenol when warmed. There is no gas evolved this time. The reaction forms an azo dye and is called a **coupling reaction** because the benzene rings are joined together by an azo (—N=N—) group (Figure 34).

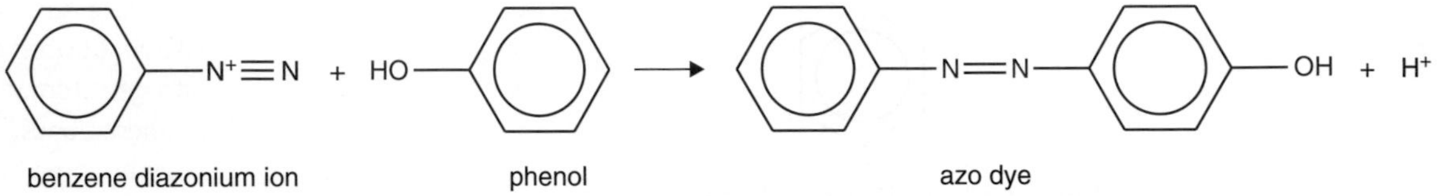

benzene diazonium ion   phenol   azo dye

Figure 34 Formation of an azo dye

The chloride ions remain in solution. The azo dye appears as a **yellow precipitate**. Azo compounds are used as indicators and dyes.

> **Examiner tip**
> Dyes (including azo dyes) and indicators are coloured because they have an extended π delocalised system that brings the electronic energy levels closer together, and so light is absorbed in the visible region of the spectrum. The name of the azo dye shown in Figure 34 is 4-hydroxyphenylazobenzene.

If a compound other than phenol is given to bond with the azo dye, attach the N=N to it anywhere on the ring where there is a hydrogen atom. Be careful of fused ring structures such as naphthalene (or naphthalen-2-ol — shown in Figure 35) because you must bond it to the N=N at any point where there is a hydrogen atom. The carbon atoms at the intersection of the rings do not have hydrogen atoms.

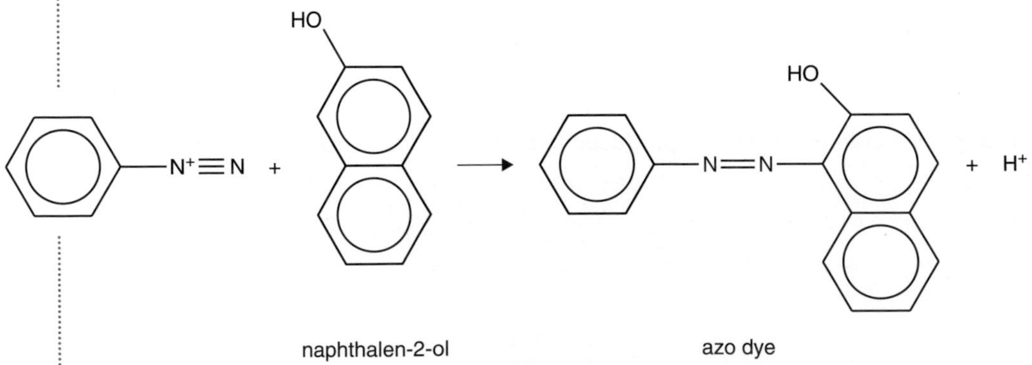

naphthalen-2-ol   azo dye

Figure 35

CCEA A2 Chemistry

Aliphatic amines with nitrous acid

The diazonium ion formed from aliphatic amines is not stable at any temperature and breaks down immediately to form the alcohol. For example:

$$CH_3CH_2NH_2 \quad + \quad HNO_2 \quad \rightarrow \quad CH_3CH_2OH \quad + \quad N_2 \quad + \quad H_2O$$

ethylamine ethanol

The amine is mixed with sodium nitrite and hydrochloric acid. Bubbles of a colourless gas (N_2) are produced immediately even when it is below 5°C.

Summary

- Amines can be classified as primary, secondary or tertiary.
- Amines react as bases with acids forming alkylammonium compounds.
- Amines are formed from substitution reactions of halogenoalkanes and reduction of nitriles and amides.
- Aromatic amines react with nitrous acid below 5°C, forming a diazonium salt, which can be used to prepare many different compounds, including azo dyes.
- Aliphatic amines react with nitrous acid, forming alcohols.

Amides

Amides contain the functional group —$CONH_2$ (Figure 36).

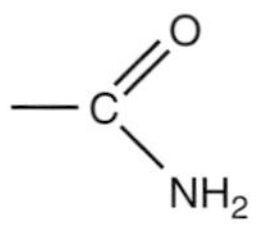

The general formula of an amide is $RCONH_2$ where R is an alkyl group.

Amides are named from the carboxylic acid; for example, methanoic acid leads to the name methanamide. If you have a substituent on the chain — for example, CH_3, CI — then you must number from the carbon atom in the amide group as you would with carboxylic acids.

Figure 36

The molecular formulae of the first six straight-chain amides are given in Table 11 with their states at room temperature and pressure. Figure 37 shows the structural formulae of ethanamide and 4-hydroxypentanamide.

Table 11

Molecular formula	Name	State at room temperature and pressure
$HCONH_2$	Methanamide	Liquid
CH_3CONH_2	Ethanamide	Solid
$CH_3CH_2CONH_2$	Propanamide	Solid
$CH_3CH_2CH_2CONH_2$	Butanamide	Solid
$CH_3CH_2CH_2CH_2CONH_2$	Pentanamide	Solid
$CH_3CH_2CH_2CH_2CH_2CONH_2$	Hexanamide	Solid

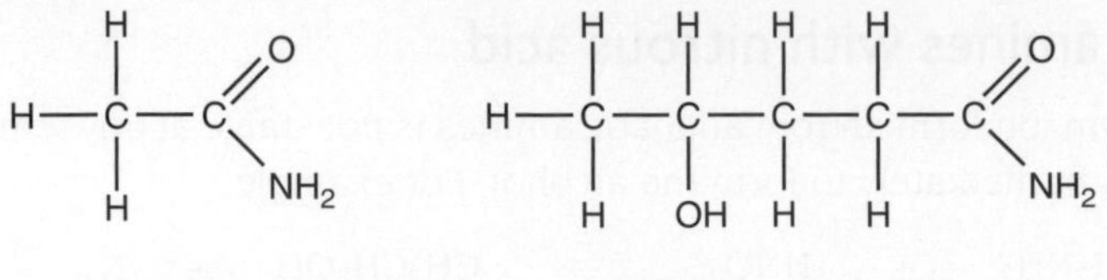

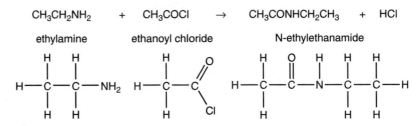

ethanamide   4-hydroxypentanamide

Figure 37

Preparation of amides

Amides are prepared in two ways.

Dehydration of an ammonium salt of a carboxylic acid

Heating an ammonium salt of a carboxylic acid causes it to dehydrate to form an amide. For example:

$$CH_3COONH_4 \rightarrow CH_3CONH_2 + H_2O$$

ammonium ethanoate   ethanamide

Acid chloride with an amine

An acid chloride reacts with an amine to form an N-substituted amide. An example is shown in Figure 38.

$$CH_3CH_2NH_2 + CH_3COCl \rightarrow CH_3CONHCH_2CH_3 + HCl$$

ethylamine   ethanoyl chloride   N-ethylethanamide

Figure 38

Hydrolysis of amides

Amides can be hydrolysed using dilute acid or dilute alkali.

Acid hydrolysis

Acid hydrolysis of an amide produces a carboxylic acid and the ammonium salt of the dilute acid. For example:

$$CH_3CONH_2 + H_2O + HCl \rightarrow CH_3COOH + NH_4Cl$$

ethanamide   ethanoic acid   ammonium chloride

$$CH_3CH_2CONH_2 \quad + \quad H_2O \quad + \quad HCl \quad \rightarrow \quad CH_3CH_2COOH \quad + \quad NH_4Cl$$

propanamide $\qquad\qquad\qquad\qquad\qquad$ propanoic acid $\qquad$ ammonium chloride

Alkaline hydrolysis

Alkaline hydrolysis of an amide produces the salt of the carboxylic acid and ammonia gas. For example:

$$CH_3CONH_2 \quad + \quad NaOH \quad \rightarrow \quad CH_3COONa \quad + \quad NH_3$$

ethanamide $\qquad\qquad\qquad\qquad\qquad$ sodium ethanoate $\qquad$ ammonia

$$CH_3CH_2CH_2CONH_2 \quad + \quad KOH \quad \rightarrow \quad CH_3CH_2CH_2COOK \quad + \quad NH_3$$

butanamide $\qquad\qquad\qquad\qquad\qquad$ potassium butanoate $\qquad$ ammonia

Examiner tip

The alkaline hydrolysis of an amide can be used as a test for an amide. Warm the solid organic compound with sodium hydroxide solution and if it is an amide it will produce ammonia gas. The ammonia gas can be tested using damp universal indicator paper (changes to blue — alkaline gas; possibly ammonia) and a glass rod dipped in concentrated hydrochloric acid (white smoke — ammonia gas released from an amide).

Examiner tip

When writing the equation for alkaline hydrolysis of an amide you only need to include the alkali (NaOH or KOH) as the reactant with the amide. Alkaline hydrolysis is often called alkaline-catalysed hydrolysis.

Dehydration of amides

Amides can be **dehydrated** by distilling them over phosphorus(v) oxide, P_4O_{10}.

When amides are dehydrated they form nitriles (functional group —C≡N — cyano group). For example:

$$CH_3CH_2CONH_2 \quad \rightarrow \quad CH_3CH_2C{\equiv}N \quad + \quad H_2O$$

propanamide $\qquad\qquad\qquad$ propanenitrile

$$CH_3CONH_2 \quad \rightarrow \quad CH_3C{\equiv}N \quad + \quad H_2O$$

ethanamide $\qquad\qquad\qquad$ ethanenitrile

The **dehydration** of an amide is a reaction that involves the elimination of water from the amide, forming a nitrile.

Basicity of amides

Amides are poor bases. This is because the delocalisation of the lone pair on the nitrogen atom makes the lone pair more stable and so less easily donated to a hydrogen ion. Amides are poorer bases than phenylamine.

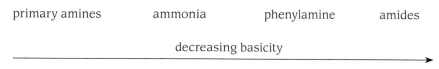

primary amines $\qquad$ ammonia $\qquad$ phenylamine $\qquad$ amides

decreasing basicity

Summary

- Amides are formed from the dehydration of ammonium salts of carboxylic acids on heating.
- Amides are further dehydrated to nitriles by distilling over phosphorus(V) oxide.
- Amides are reduced to primary amines using lithal in dry ether.

- Amides are hydrolysed forming the carboxylic acid and ammonia.
- In acid hydrolysis the carboxylic acid and the ammonium salt of the dilute acid are formed.
- In alkaline hydrolysis the carboxylic acid salt and ammonia are formed. The formation of ammonia on alkaline hydrolysis can be used to identify an amide.

Amino acids

An amino acid contains an NH_2 group and a COOH group. An α-amino acid has an NH_2 group and a COOH group attached to the same carbon atom. The general structure of an amino acid is shown in Figure 39.

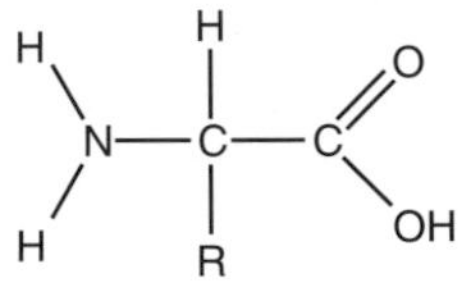

Figure 39 General structure of an amino acid

Examiner tip

The systematic name for glycine is aminoethanoic acid and for alanine it is 2-aminopropanoic acid. This is important when naming the salts of these amino acids.

If R is H, the amino acid is glycine. If R is CH_3, the amino acid is alanine. Glycine is not optically active; alanine is optically active.

The two groups are in equilibrium with H^+ ions:

(a) $-NH_2$ + H^+ $\rightleftharpoons$ $-NH_3^+$

(b) $-COOH$ $\rightleftharpoons$ $-COO^-$ + H^+

The equilibria are altered in acidic and alkaline solution. In *acidic* solution, there is a large concentration of H^+ ions:

- equilibrium (a) is pushed to the right-hand side
- equilibrium (b) is pushed to the left-hand side

The structure of the amino acid at low pH is shown in Figure 40.

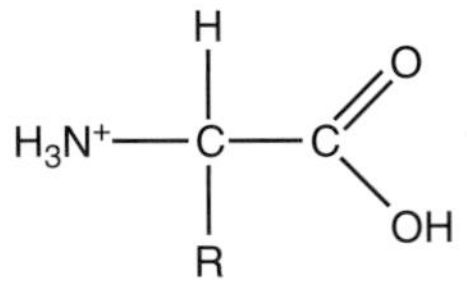

Figure 40 Amino acid at low pH

In *alkaline* solution, there is a low concentration of H^+ ions:

- equilibrium (a) is pushed to the left-hand side
- equilibrium (b) is pushed to the right-hand side

The structure of the amino acid at high pH is shown in Figure 41.

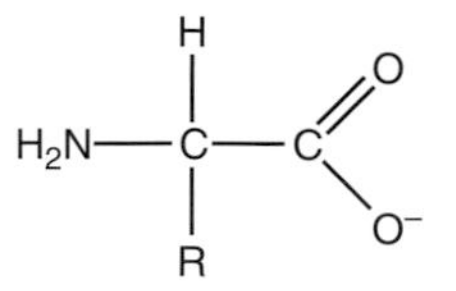

Figure 41 Amino acid at high pH

At a certain pH (i.e. the isoelectric point) the amino acid exists as a dipolar ion (Figure 42). This dipolar ion is also called a **zwitterion**.

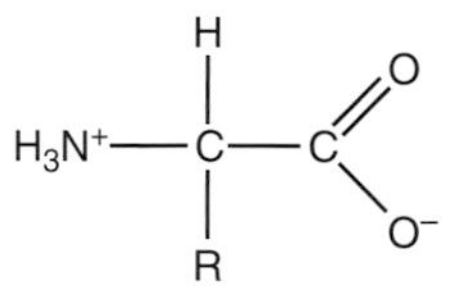

Figure 42 Zwitterion structure

Zwitterions have a permanent positive and negative charge but are neutral overall.

Knowledge check 19

Explain why glycine is not optically active.

Physical properties of amino acids

- Amino acids have *high melting points* (they are solids at room temperature and pressure).
- Amino acids exist as dipolar ions. The attraction between these ions is strong and requires a lot of energy to overcome. This gives amino acids a high melting point.
- Amino acids are *soluble in water*.
- Amino acids exist as dipolar ions. These ions can interact with polar water molecules, and this allows them to dissolve in water.

Chemical properties of amino acids

The reactions of amino acids involve the reaction of the COOH group or the NH_2 group, or of the whole molecule.

Reaction of amino acids with sodium carbonate

These reactions occur at the COOH group.

Glycine (H_2NCH_2COOH):

$$2H_2NCH_2COOH + Na_2CO_3 \rightarrow 2H_2NCH_2COONa + CO_2 + H_2O$$

glycine   sodium aminoethanoate

Observations: bubbles of a colourless gas evolved (CO_2)

Alanine ($H_2NCH(CH_3)COOH$):

$$2H_2NCH(CH_3)COOH + Na_2CO_3 \rightarrow 2H_2NCH(CH_3)COONa + CO_2 + H_2O$$

alanine   sodium 2-aminopropanoate

Observations: bubbles of a colourless gas evolved (CO_2)

Reaction of amino acids with nitrous acid, HNO_2

Nitrous acid is formed in situ from sodium nitrite and hydrochloric acid. Amino acids react as aliphatic amines at the NH_2 group. The NH_2 group is converted into an OH group.

Glycine (H_2NCH_2COOH):

$$H_2NCH_2COOH \quad + \quad HNO_2 \quad \rightarrow \quad HOCH_2COOH \quad + \quad N_2 \quad + \quad H_2O$$

glycine   hydroxyethanoic acid

Observations: bubbles of a colourless gas evolved (N_2)

Alanine ($H_2NCH(CH_3)COOH$):

$$H_2NCH(CH_3)COOH \quad + \quad HNO_2 \quad \rightarrow \quad HOCH(CH_3)COOH \quad + \quad N_2 \quad + \quad H_2O$$

alanine   2-hydroxypropanoic acid

Observations: bubbles of a colourless gas evolved (N_2)

Reaction of glycine with copper(II) sulfate, $CuSO_4$

A complex is formed with a coordination number of 4. Glycine acts as a bidentate ligand.

Glycine (H_2NCH_2COOH):

$$Cu^{2+}(aq) \quad + \quad 2H_2NCH_2COOH \quad \rightarrow \quad [Cu(H_2NCH_2COOH)_2]^{2+}$$

copper(II)-glycine

Observations: dark blue solution formed when solutions of copper(II) sulfate and glycine are mixed

Formation of peptides

Amino acids react together in a condensation polymerisation reaction to form peptides (which contain a peptide group). An example is shown in Figure 43.

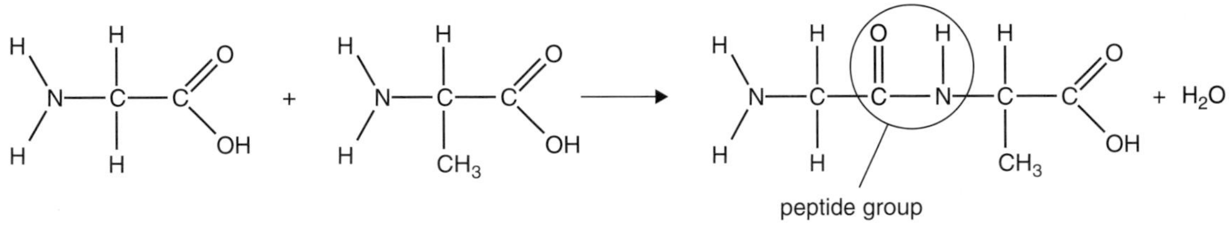

peptide group

Figure 43 Formation of a dipeptide

- The peptide formed is called a dipeptide because it contains two amino acid residues.
- Peptides can be hydrolysed.

- Acid-catalysed hydrolysis of a peptide produces positive amino acid ions containing —NH_3^+.
- Alkaline-catalysed hydrolysis of a peptide produces negative amino acid ions containing —COO^-.

Proteins

Proteins have different levels of structure.

- The **primary structure** of a protein is the sequence of amino acids produced by condensation reactions forming peptide groups (often called peptide bonds) between amino acids.
- The **secondary structure** of a protein is the twisting/coiling of the protein chain to form α-helix/β-pleated sheet held together by intramolecular hydrogen bonds between the C=O and N—H groups.
- The **tertiary structure** of a protein is the final bending/folding of the structure of the protein to give a precise three-dimensional shape held together by ionic interactions of ionic groups such as the NH_3^+ and COO^- of side chains, hydrogen bonds between side groups, disulfide bridges (—S—S—), and hydrophobic and hydrophilic interactions and van der Waals forces between side groups.

Functions of proteins

Proteins have many functional and structural roles in organisms. Some proteins are **enzymes, which are biological catalysts**. Enzymes function by providing an active site in the enzyme molecule. The substrate (or reactant) binds to the active site forming an enzyme–substrate complex. The groups in the active site catalyse the reaction. The products leave the active site and the enzyme is regenerated.

The substrate fits into the active site like a key into a lock. No other substrate will fit into the active site. For optically active molecules only one of the optical isomers can be a substrate for the enzyme.

Enzyme function is temperature dependent. Enzymes have an optimum temperature when their function is at its maximum. At higher temperatures enzymes are denatured, which means that the coiling and folding of the protein break down. The peptide bonds do not break above this temperature.

Enzymes also have an optimum pH. The enzyme again denatures when the pH is altered because the equilibrium of NH_2 and COOH groups alters, changing the bonding. Again peptides bonds are not broken.

Examiner tip

The side chain (R group) of amino acids can be non-polar, polar, positively charged, negatively charged and sulfur containing. Much of the tertiary structure of a protein is caused by the interactions between these groups. Non-polar R groups are hydrophobic (water hating) and tend to avoid contact with the aqueous environment in which the proteins are found, whereas polar and ionic R groups are hydrophilic (water loving) and interact with the aqueous environment. Sulfur-containing R groups can bond to form disulfide bridges.

Knowledge check 20

Describe the primary structure of a protein.

The **active site** is the site on the surface of the enzyme into which the substrate fits.

- Amino acids contain an acid group (COOH) and an amino group (NH_2).
- Alpha (α) amino acids have the COOH group and the NH_2 group bonded to the same carbon atom.
- Most amino acids are optically active, but glycine is not.
- Amino acids react with sodium carbonate, nitrous acid and copper(ii) sulfate solution.
- Amino acids form polymers called polypeptides.
- Proteins have a primary, secondary and tertiary structure.

Summary

A **polymer** is a large molecule consisting of many repeating monomer units joined together.

A **monomer** is a small molecule. Monomer molecules join together to form a long chain called a polymer.

Polymers

Two main types of **polymers** are considered here:
- addition polymers
- condensation polymers

Addition polymerisation

Addition polymerisation occurs between alkene molecules. Alkenes react with other alkene molecules to form polymers that are commonly used as plastics.

Polythene or poly(ethene)

Polythene is formed when ethene molecules add to each other to form a chain of carbon atoms. The unit that breaks its double bond is called the **monomer** and the long chain formed is called the polymer. This can be represented by the equation shown in Figure 44.

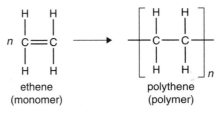

Figure 44

Types of polythene

There are two main types of polythene:
- low-density polythene, LD polythene (LDPE)
- high-density polythene, HD polythene (HDPE)

The level of side branching in HD and LD polythene differs. The degree of branching controls the degree of van der Waals forces between polymer molecules. The higher the degree of branching the fewer the van der Waals forces. This results in a lower softening temperature (T_m) for the polymer.

Less branching in a polymer molecule results in greater interaction between molecules. This causes increased van der Waals forces between molecules and so greater crystallinity in the structure of the polymer. Greater crystallinity results in less flexibility in structure. Figure 45 shows diagrams representing the structure of the two forms of polythene. Table 12 summarises their properties.

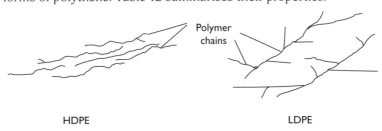

Figure 45 Structures of HDPE and LDPE

CCEA A2 Chemistry

Table 12

HDPE	LDPE
Highly unbranched chains allow a more regular structure and greater contact between the polymer chains	Highly branched chains make a less regular structure and allow less contact between the polymer chains
The regular structure leads to a more crystalline structure	A less regular structure leads to a less crystalline structure
Greater crystallinity leads to reduced flexibility	Lower crystallinity leads to increased flexibility
More contact between the polymer chains leads to greater van der Waals forces of attraction and so to a higher T_m	Less contact between the polymer chains leads to fewer van der Waals forces of attraction and so a lower T_m

Conditions for the formation of LDPE and HDPE

Table 13 shows the conditions for the formation of both LD and HD polythene, and the main uses for each type. It also gives a summary of their properties.

Table 13

	LD polythene (LDPE)	HD polythene (HDPE)
Temperature	100–300°C (high)	50–75°C (low)
Pressure	1000–2000 atm (high)	1–10 atm (low)
Catalyst	None	Ziegler catalyst (triethylaluminium and titanium(IV) chloride)
Uses	Plastic bags/toys	Food boxes, buckets, kitchenware, bowls
Branching	High	Low
Crystallinity	Low	High
Flexibility	High	Low
T_m	Low	High

Examiner tip

The conditions in terms of temperature and pressure are very specific, but low and high are often acceptable without quoted values. The details of the Ziegler catalyst are important and should be described in detail.

The equation of the formation of any addition polymer is based on the formation of polythene. The double bond is broken and other molecules are added to either side. An example is shown in Figure 46.

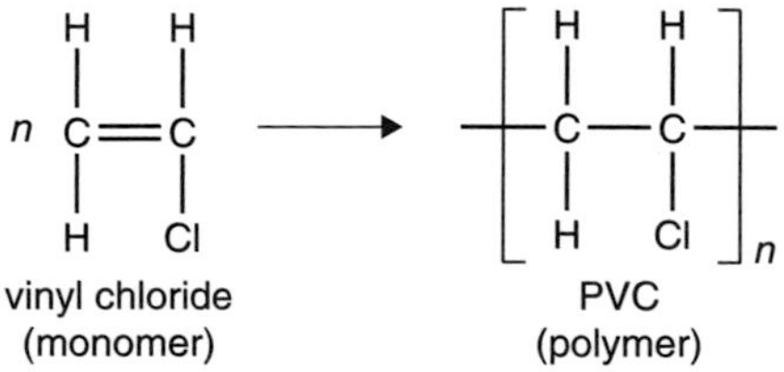

vinyl chloride (monomer) → PVC (polymer)

Figure 46 Polymerisation of vinyl chloride

Vinyl chloride is also called chloroethene and the polymer is often called poly(chloroethene). The chloroethene is placed in brackets to show that the polymer is formed from chloroethene. The correct chemical name of polythene is poly(ethene).

Disposal of polythene

Polythene is a useful material but it is chemically inert and is non-biodegradable and so represents an environmental problem in its disposal. There are two major ways to dispose of polythene:

- landfill
- incineration

Neither landfill nor incineration is a suitable method of disposal. The burial of tonnes of polythene in landfill sites does not help in breaking them down and they will still be there in thousands of years.

The incineration of polythene produces carbon dioxide and water. Carbon dioxide is a significant greenhouse gas. Incineration prevents unsightly landfill sites in the countryside and the energy produced by the combustion of the polymers can be used to generate electricity.

Governments must develop a strategy for recycling as many polymers as possible, including polythene, and plastic objects should be replaced with more environmentally friendly alternatives such as paper bags from sustainable forests.

Condensation polymerisation

Molecules that possess COOH and OH groups or COOH and NH_2 groups can form **condensation polymers**. During the formation of a condensation polymer, water or HCl is eliminated.

A **condensation polymer** is a polymer formed when monomers join together and eliminate a small molecule such as water or hydrogen chloride.

Two types of condensation polymer are considered here:

- polyesters
- polyamides

Polyesters

A polyester is a condensation polymer formed between a diol and a dicarboxylic acid (or between molecules of a single compound that contains both a COOH group and an OH group). The reaction is described as condensation polymerisation because it eliminates water. This is in contrast to the addition polymerisation of ethene to form polythene.

One polyester is formed from the reaction between ethane-1,2-diol and benzene-1,4-dicarboxylic acid (terephthalic acid) — see Figure 47. The polyester is called poly(ethylene terephthalate) or PET (sometimes PETE).

Examiner tip
PET is a polyester because it contains many ester (COO) groups.

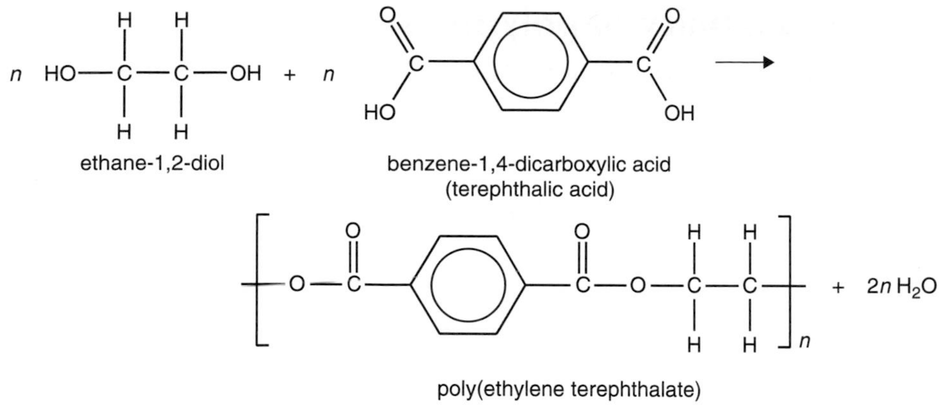

Figure 47 Formation of a polyester

Examiner tip

Note that two waters are eliminated for the formation of one repeating unit since one repeating unit has two ester groups (COO) and the formation of each one eliminates a molecule of water.

Polyamides

Nylon is a condensation polymer formed from the reaction between hexane-1,6-diamine (also called 1,6-diaminohexane) and adipic acid (hexane dioic acid) — see Figure 48. Nylon is used to make ropes, fishing nets and some garments such as tights.

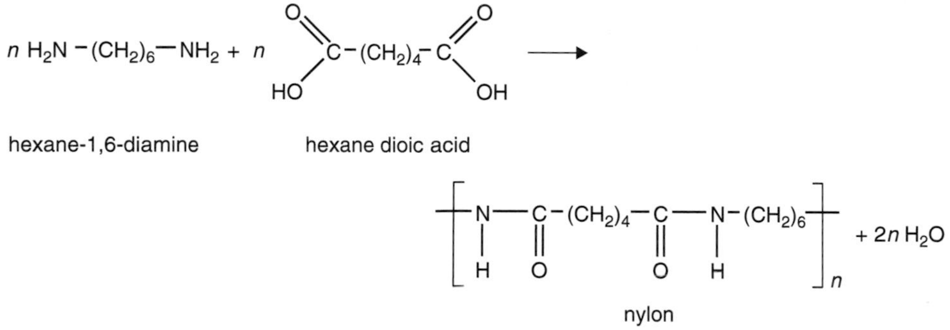

Figure 48 Formation of nylon using hexane dioic acid

A diacyl dichloride (a molecule containing two acid chloride (COCl) groups) can be used in place of the dioic acid and the elimination product is HCl rather than water (Figure 49).

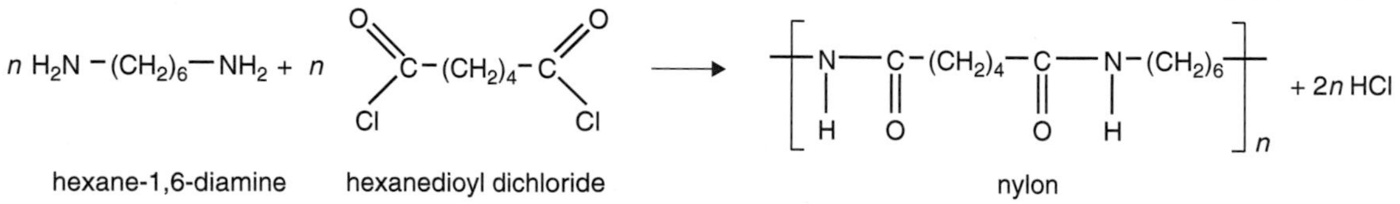

Figure 49 Formation of nylon using a diacyl dichloride

Examiner tip

A polyester could be formed using a diacyl dichloride (a molecule containing two acid chloride groups) and a diol. In that case 2HCl would be eliminated.

Examiner tip

Nylon is a polyamide because it contains many amide groups (CONH).

Examiner tip

This form of nylon is often called nylon-6,6 because it is made from a diamine containing six carbon atoms and a dioic acid containing six carbon atoms. Nylon-6,10 also exists where the dioic acid contains ten carbon atoms.

Examiner tip

Hexanedioyl dichloride is often called adipoyl chloride from the common name of the dioic acid. Sebacic acid is the common name for decane-1,10-dioic acid and the acid chloride is often called sebacoyl chloride. Sebacoyl chloride is often used in the nylon rope trick, forming nylon from the boundary between layers of sebacoyl chloride and 1,6-diaminohexane.

Knowledge check 22

Name one condensation polymer.

Biodegradability of polymers

A **biodegradable** polymer is one that can be broken down in the environment by the action of microorganisms.

Condensation polymers can be hydrolysed and so are now being used more than addition polymers. This means that they are **biodegradable** in the environment. Many drinks bottles, especially water bottles, are now made from PET.

Addition polymers such as polythene will remain for thousands of years in the environment but PET can be hydrolysed by microorganisms in the environment, so it biodegrades.

Summary

- There are two main types of polymer: addition and condensation.
- Polythene and PVC are addition polymers formed from addition reactions of alkenes.
- There are two forms of polythene: high-density polythene (HDPE) and low-density polythene (LDPE).
- PET and nylon are condensation polymers formed from condensation (elimination) reactions.
- Condensation polymers are biodegradable.

Organic identification tests

The organic identification tests summarised in Table 14 are useful in practical examinations and in describing tests for organic compounds. Tests 1–8 are used in AS chemistry. Tests 9–18 are used in A2 chemistry. Since A2 chemistry is synoptic, the AS tests can appear in both AS and A2.

Table 14

Test and testing for	How to carry out the test	Typical observations	Deductions from observations
(1) Appearance and smell	Observe colour and state; smell cautiously	Colourless liquid with characteristic spirit/alcohol smell	Possibly an alcohol/ethanol
		Colourless liquid with a sharp, irritating smell	Possibly a carboxylic acid/ ethanoic acid
		Fruity/sweet/solvent-like smell	Possibly an ester
(2) Miscibility/solubility in water Testing for polarity of the liquid/ionic nature of the solid	Add a few cm^3 of the liquid to deionised water in a test tube or Add a spatula measure of the solid (usually an amino acid) to a few cm^3 of deionised water in a test tube	Liquid mixes with water/one layer or Solid dissolves in water and colourless solution forms	Polar liquid — possibly an alcohol/carboxylic acid/short-carbon-chain aldehyde or ketone or Ionic compound/amino acid
		Liquid does not mix with water/ two layers formed or Solid does not dissolve in water	Non-polar liquid or Not an ionic compound
(3) Combustion Testing for carbon content	Place a few drops of the liquid on a watch glass and ignite with a lit splint	Clean blue flame	Low carbon content/possibly an alcohol
		Sooty orange flame	High carbon content/possibly an alkane/alkene/long-chain alcohol

Test and testing for	How to carry out the test	Typical observations	Deductions from observations
(4) Bromine water Testing for presence of C=C/alkene	Add a few cm³ of bromine water to the liquid or solution in a test tube	Bromine water changes from orange to colourless	C=C/alkene present
		Orange colour of bromine water remains	No C=C present
(5) Silver nitrate solution with ethanol Testing for presence of halogen atoms in a halogenoalkane	Add 1 cm³ of the halogenoalkane to a few cm³ of ethanol; add silver nitrate solution and warm in a water bath	White precipitate (slow to form)	Chloroalkane
		Cream precipitate (forms faster than white precipitate)	Bromoalkane
		Yellow precipitate (forms reasonably fast)	Iodoalkane
(6) Phosphorus pentachloride (PCl_5) Testing for an OH/alcohol group	To a few cm³ of the liquid add a few crystals of PCl_5 Test any gas released with a glass rod dipped in concentrated ammonia (NH_3) solution	Gas released; misty fumes; solid disappears; heat released; white smoke with concentrated ammonia solution	Alcohol/OH group present; HCl gas released; white smoke is ammonium chloride (NH_4Cl)
		No gas released; no white smoke with concentrated ammonia solution	Not an alcohol/no OH group present
(7) Acidified potassium dichromate Testing for a primary/ secondary alcohol as opposed to a tertiary alcohol	Mix a few cm³ of the liquid or solution with acidified potassium dichromate solution in a test tube and warm in a water bath	Orange solution changes to green Change in smell	Primary or secondary alcohol group (OH) present Can be oxidised
		Solution remains orange	Tertiary alcohol group (OH) present Cannot be oxidised
(8) Iodoform test Testing for a $CH_3CH(OH)$ group in an alcohol	To a few cm³ of the liquid add sodium hydroxide solution and iodine solution and warm	Yellow precipitate	$CH_3CH(OH)$ group present
		No yellow precipitate	No $CH_3CH(OH)$ group present
(9) Sodium carbonate (Na_2CO_3) or sodium hydrogen carbonate ($NaHCO_3$) Testing for the COOH group in a carboxylic acid or the COOH group in an amino acid	To a few cm³ of the liquid add half a spatula measure of solid Na_2CO_3 or $NaHCO_3$ or To a few cm³ of Na_2CO_3 solution or $NaHCO_3$ solution add the organic solid	Gas released; solid disappears; bubble gas through limewater and it changes from colourless to milky	Carboxylic acid/COOH group present; CO_2 gas released
		No gas released	Not a carboxylic acid/no COOH group present
(10) Magnesium Testing for a carboxylic acid (or a COOH group in an amino acid)	To a few cm³ of the liquid add a strip of magnesium ribbon	Gas released; magnesium disappears; test gas with lit splint — pop sound	Carboxylic acid/COOH group present; H_2 gas released
		No gas released	Not a carboxylic acid/no COOH group present

Continued

Test and testing for	How to carry out the test	Typical observations	Deductions from observations
(11) Phosphorus pentachloride (PCl$_5$) Testing for a carboxylic acid/COOH group	To a few cm^3 of the liquid add a few crystals of PCl$_5$; test any gas released with a glass rod dipped in concentrated ammonia (NH$_3$) solution	Gas released; misty fumes; solid disappears; heat released; white smoke with concentrated ammonia solution	Carboxylic acid/COOH group present; HCl gas released; white smoke is ammonium chloride (NH$_4$Cl)
		No gas released; no white smoke with concentrated ammonia solution	Not a carboxylic acid/no COOH group present
(12) 2,4-dinitrophenylhydrazine Testing for a C$=$O group in aldehydes and ketones	Add a few drops of the liquid to a few cm^3 of the 2,4-dinitrophenylhydrazine solution in a test tube	Yellow/orange precipitate	C$=$O group present in an aldehyde or ketone/aldehyde or ketone present
		No yellow/orange precipitate	No C$=$O group in an aldehyde or ketone/not an aldehyde or ketone
(13) Acidified potassium dichromate solution Distinguishing between an aldehyde and a ketone	Mix a few cm^3 of the liquid or solution with acidified potassium dichromate solution in a test tube and warm in a water bath	Orange solution changes to green	Aldehyde/CHO group present Can be oxidised
		Solution remains orange	Not an aldehyde/no CHO group present/ketone Cannot be oxidised
(14) Fehling's solution Distinguishing between an aldehyde and a ketone	Mix Fehling's solution 1 and Fehling's solution 2 in a test tube. Add a few cm^3 of the resulting solution to the liquid in a test tube and warm in a water bath	Blue solution changes to give a red precipitate	Aldehyde/CHO group present
		Solution remains blue	Not an aldehyde/no CHO group present/ketone
(15) Tollens' reagent Distinguishing between an aldehyde and a ketone	Mix a few cm^3 of the liquid with ammonia and silver nitrate solution in a test tube and warm in a water bath	Colourless solution changes to give a silver mirror	Aldehyde/CHO group present
		Solution remains colourless	Not an aldehyde/no CHO group present/ketone
(16) Amide test Testing for the presence of an amide	Mix the solid/liquid with sodium hydroxide solution and warm Test any gas released with a glass rod dipped in concentrated hydrochloric acid	Gas released; white smoke with concentrated hydrochloric acid	Ammonia gas released from an amide; white smoke with concentrated HCl is ammonium chloride (NH$_4$Cl)
		No gas released; no white smoke with concentrated hydrochloric acid	No ammonia gas so substance is not an amide
(17) Amino group test Testing for the presence of an amino group (NH$_2$) in an amine or amino acid	Place a few cm^3 of concentrated hydrochloric acid in a test tube and add sodium nitrite solution; wait until effervescence stops; add this solution to a solution of the amine or amino acid in water and warm gently in a water bath	Rapid effervescence	NH$_2$ group present
		No effervescence	No NH$_2$ group present

Test and testing for	How to carry out the test	Typical observations	Deductions from observations
(18) Copper(II) sulfate solution Testing for glycine	Add a few cm³ of a solution of copper sulfate to a solution of the solid	Deep blue solution	Glycine present; forms copper(II) glycine complex
		No change	No glycine present; no complex formed

Organic reactions of homologous series

Figure 50 shows the main organic reactions of homologous series in the whole CCEA A-level course. You should know the reagents used for each reaction including any conditions, any relevant mechanisms and the type of reaction. You should also be able to name reactants and products and write equations for the reactions. Oxidation and reduction reactions may be presented using [O] and [H] respectively.

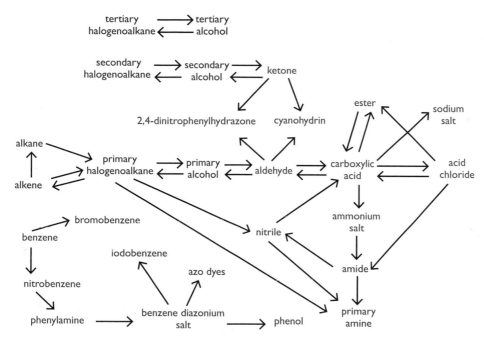

Figure 50 The main organic reactions of homologous series for CCEA A-level chemistry.
Blue = AS Unit 2, purple = A2 Unit 1, red = A2 Unit 2

Examiner tip
POACHERS is a good way to remember some of the main types of organic reactions.
P = polymerisation, O = oxidation, A = addition, C = condensation, H = hydrolysis, E = elimination, R = reduction, S = substitution.

Questions & Answers

The unit test

The A2 Unit 2 examination is 2 hours in length and consists of 10 multiple-choice questions (each worth 2 marks) and several structured questions, which vary in length. The structured questions make up the remaining 100 marks giving 120 marks in total for the paper. For each multiple-choice question there is one correct answer and at least one very clear distractor.

About this section

Answers to some questions are followed by examiner comments. These are preceded by the icon  and provide brief guidance on how to approach the question and also where you could make errors. You could try the questions first to see how you get on and then check the answers and comments.

Mass spectrometry and nmr spectroscopy

Question I

The mass spectrum of ethanamide, CH_3CONH_2, is shown below.

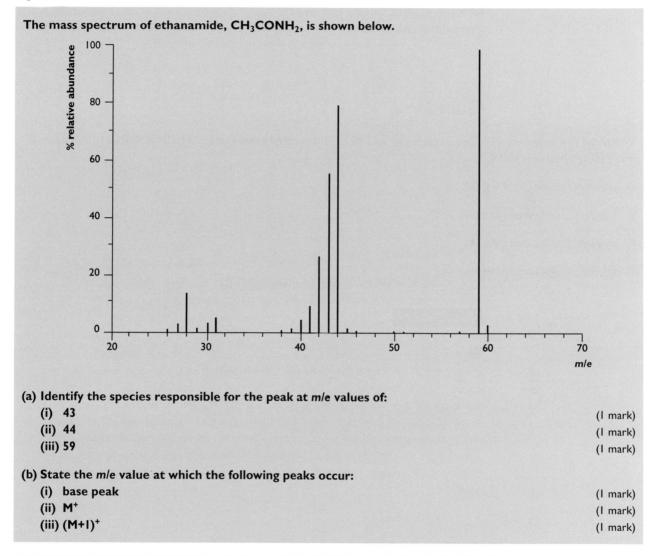

(a) Identify the species responsible for the peak at m/e values of:

  (i) 43   (1 mark)

  (ii) 44   (1 mark)

  (iii) 59   (1 mark)

(b) State the m/e value at which the following peaks occur:

  (i) base peak   (1 mark)

  (ii) M^+ (1 mark)

  (iii) $(M+I)^+$ (1 mark)

(a)   **(i)** CH_3CO^+ ✓

    (ii) $CONH_2^+$ ✓

    (iii) $CH_3CONH_2^+$ ✓

(e) Sketch out the structure of the molecule and determine which part of the molecule would give the correct mass of a fragment. The species that cause the peaks always have a single positive charge.

(b) (i) 59 ✓
    (ii) 59 ✓
    (iii) 60 ✓

(e) In this example the base peak and the molecular ion peak occur at the same m/e value. This means that the molecular ion is the most abundant ion in the mass spectrum of ethanamide. The $(M+1)^+$ peak occurs at an m/e value 1 greater than the M^+ peak.

Question 2

Which of the following splitting patterns would be seen for ethyl ethanoate, $CH_3CH_2OOCCH_3$, in order of increasing chemical shift?

A **quartet, singlet and triplet**

B **singlet, quartet and triplet**

C **singlet, triplet and quartet**

D **triplet, singlet and quartet**

Answer is D

(e) There are three environments of chemically equivalent hydrogen atoms in ethyl ethanoate (CH_3, CH_2 and CH_3). The most deshielded will be the environment closest to the electronegative oxygen, which is the CH_2 (split by a CH_3), resulting in a quartet; so the quartet will be the most deshielded and so at the highest chemical shift value. The CH_3 group bonded to the CO will be the next most deshielded and this signal will not be split as there are no hydrogen atoms bonded to adjacent carbon atoms; this will be a singlet. The final CH_3 group (appearing as a triplet due to the CH_2 group) is the least deshielded as it is furthest from the electronegative oxygen. The order is therefore, in increasing chemical shift: triplet, singlet, quartet.

Question 3

The following ¹H nmr spectrum is for a compound with molecular formula C₄H₉Br.

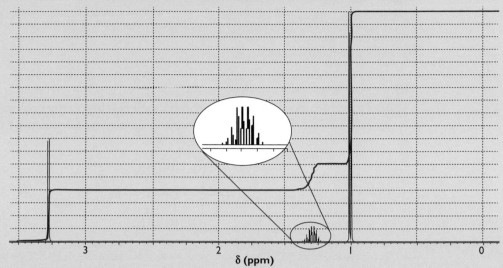

δ (ppm)

(a) Draw and name four molecules that have the molecular formula C₄H₉Br. (4 marks)

(b) Explain why there is a signal at δ = 0 ppm. (1 mark)

(c) State the number of chemical environments of hydrogen atoms in the spectrum shown. (1 mark)

(d) State the number of hydrogen atoms in each environment in **(c)** based on the integration. (1 mark)

(e) Explain the spin–spin splitting pattern for each environment. (3 marks)

(f) State which of the molecules you have drawn in **(a)** would give this nmr spectrum. (1 mark)

(a)

1-bromobutane   ✓

2-bromobutane   ✓

2-bromo-2-methylpropane   ✓

1-bromo-2-methylpropane   ✓

(b) Signal at δ = 0 is for TMS (tetramethylsilane), which is used as a standard. ✓
(c) 3 ✓

(d) Ratio is 12:2:4 = 6:1:2 ✓

(e)

Doublet at $\delta = 1.0$	*One* hydrogen atom bonded to adjacent carbon atoms ✓
Nonet at $\delta = 1.3$	*Eight* hydrogen atoms bonded to adjacent carbon atoms ✓
Doublet at $\delta = 3.5$	*One* hydrogen atom bonded to adjacent carbon atoms ✓

(f) 1-bromo-2-methylpropane ✓

🄴 1-bromopropane and 2-bromopropane would both have four environments of chemically equivalent hydrogen atoms. 2-bromo-2-methylpropane would have one environment of chemically equivalent hydrogen atoms. 1-bromo-2-methylpropane would have three environments of chemically equivalent hydrogen atoms.

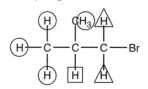

All six hydrogen atoms circled are in one environment — they are split by a single hydrogen atom (shown in a square) bonded to the adjacent carbon atom — this gives a doublet. The single hydrogen atom in the square is split by eight hydrogen atoms bonded to adjacent carbon atoms — this gives a nonet. The signal for the two hydrogen atoms (in triangles) is split by the single hydrogen (in the square) — this gives another doublet; the signal for this environment would be the most deshielded as it is closest to the electronegative bromine atom.

Volumetric analysis

Question 1

A sample of hard water contains dissolved calcium ions. 25.0 cm³ of the solution was titrated with 0.015 M edta solution in a pH 10 buffer. 17.0 cm³ of the edta solution was required.

Calculate the concentration of calcium ions in the hard water in mg dm⁻³. (3 marks)

moles of edta used = $\dfrac{17 \times 0.015}{1000}$ = 0.000255

moles of Ca^{2+} in 25.0 cm³ = 0.000255 ✓

concentration of Ca^{2+} in mol dm⁻³ = 0.000255 × 40 = 0.0102 mol dm⁻³

concentration of Ca^{2+} in g dm⁻³ = 0.0102 × 40 = 0.408 g dm⁻³ ✓

concentration of Ca^{2+} in mg dm⁻³ = 0.408 × 1000 = 408 mg dm⁻³ ✓

🄴 At A2 calculations are often set that involve the use of unusual units such as milligrams (mg) or even micrograms (μg). Make sure that you can convert between grams and milligrams.

Mistakes are often made when deciding whether to multiply by 1000 or divide by 1000. Always remember that milligrams are smaller than grams, so there will be more of them. You should therefore multiply by 1000 to convert from grams to milligrams.

The calculation here involves a 1:1 ratio of the Ca^{2+} ions to the $edta^{4-}$. The concentration of Ca^{2+} ions is determined by multiplying the moles of Ca^{2+} ion in $25\,cm^3$ by 40 to convert to $mol\,dm^{-3}$, then again by 40 to convert to $g\,dm^{-3}$ of Ca^{2+} ions and finally multiplying by 1000 to convert to $mg\,dm^{-3}$. The most common mistakes in this type of question would be using an incorrect ratio or dividing by 1000 instead of multiplying by 1000 to determine the concentration in $mg\,dm^{-3}$.

Question 2

A solution of sodium thiosulfate is prepared by dissolving 3.72 g of sodium thiosulfate, $Na_2S_2O_3.xH_2O$, in 1 dm^3 of deionised water.

25.0 cm^3 of a 0.0025 M solution of potassium iodate(v), KIO_3, is placed in a conical flask. 5 cm^3 of dilute sulfuric acid and an excess of solid potassium iodide are added. The following reaction occurs:

$$IO_3^- + 6H^+ + 5I^- \rightarrow 3H_2O + 3I_2$$

The iodine produced in the first reaction is titrated with sodium thiosulfate solution with starch indicator added near the end-point.

The average titre for this titration is 25.0 cm^3.

(a) Calculate the number of moles of iodine produced in the conical flask. (1 mark)

(b) Write a balanced symbol equation for the reaction between sodium thiosulfate and iodine. (1 mark)

(c) Calculate the mass of anhydrous sodium thiosulfate present in 1 dm^3 of solution. (1 mark)

(d) Calculate the value of x in $Na_2S_2O_3.xH_2O$. (1 mark)

(a)

$$\text{moles of potassium iodate(v) used} = \frac{25 \times 0.0025}{1000} = 6.25 \times 10^{-5}\,mol$$

moles of iodine $= 6.25 \times 10^{-5} \times 3 = 1.875 \times 10^{-4}$ ✓

(b) $2Na_2S_2O_3 + I_2 \rightarrow 2NaI + Na_2S_4O_6$ ✓

(c) $1.875 \times 10^{-4} \times 2 \times 40 = 0.015$ ✓

(d)

RFM of $Na_2S_2O_3.xH_2O = \dfrac{3.72}{0.015} = 248$

RFM of $Na_2S_2O_3 = 158$

value of $x = \dfrac{248 - 158}{18} = 5$ ✓

Question 3

2.0 g of an unknown salt of oxalic acid, $M_2C_2O_4$, were placed in a beaker and dissolved in deionised water. The solution was placed in a 250 cm³ volumetric flask and the volume made up to 250.0 cm³ using deionised water. A 25.0 cm³ portion of this solution was pipetted into a conical flask and the flask was heated to 80°C in a water bath. The heated contents were then titrated against 0.05 M acidified potassium manganate(VII) solution and the average titre was found to be 11.95 cm³. Determine the identity of the unknown salt. (4 marks)

$$2MnO_4^- + 16H^+ + 5C_2O_4^{2-} \rightarrow 2Mn^{2+} + 8H_2O + 10CO_2$$

moles of potassium manganate(VII) $= \dfrac{\text{sol vol} \times \text{conc}}{1000} = \dfrac{11.95 \times 0.05}{1000} = 0.0005975$ ✓

ratio $MnO_4^-:C_2O_4^{2-} = 2:5$

so

moles of $C_2O_4^{2-} = \dfrac{0.0005975}{2} \times 5 = 0.00149$ ✓

moles of $C_2O_4^{2-}$ in 250.0 cm³ = moles in 25.0 cm³ × 10

$= 0.00149 \times 10 = 0.0149$

$RFM = \dfrac{\text{mass}}{\text{moles}} = \dfrac{2.0}{0.0149} = 134$ ✓

RFM of $M_2C_2O_4 = 134$

RFM of $C_2O_4 = 88$

RFM of $M_2 = 134 - 88 = 46$

RAM of M = 23/salt is $Na_2C_2O_4$ ✓

e It is important to use the ratio of $MnO_4^-:C_2O_4^{2-}$ in the expression and then the rest of the calculation is carried out as normal. Volumetric calculations were first met in AS Unit 1 and the basic method is the same.

Remember that manganate(VII) titrations are self-indicating with the colour change of colourless to pink at the end-point.

Colorimetry and chromatography

Question 1

The graph below shows the change in colour intensity when a 0.02 M solution of a metal ion Y and a 0.08 M solution of a ligand Z are mixed in different volumes.

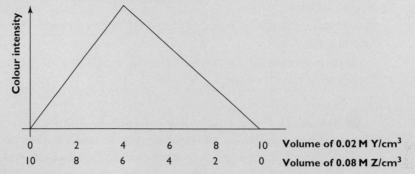

The formula of the complex formed is:

A YZ

B YZ_2

C YZ_4

D YZ_6

Answer is D

ⓔ Choose the volumes at the maximum colour intensity. The number of moles of the metal ion and the ligand are calculated and the simplest ratio of the metal ion to the ligand determined:

$$\text{moles of Y} = \frac{4 \times 0.02}{1000} = 8 \times 10^{-5}$$

$$\text{moles of Z} = \frac{6 \times 0.08}{1000} = 4.8 \times 10^{-4}$$

The simplest ratio of Y:Z is 1:6 at the maximum colour intensity.

Question 2

Explain how two-way paper chromatography could be used to separate a mixture of amino acids and detect the presence of alanine in the mixture. (5 marks)

Draw two pencil lines at 90° to each other close to the edge of a square of paper and place a concentrated spot of the solution of the amino acid mixture at the origin. ✓

Run the chromatogram in the first named solvent. ✓

Allow the chromatogram to dry and rotate through 90° and run in the second named solvent. ✓

Develop the chromatogram using ultraviolet light or a chemical developing agent (ninhydrin). ✓

Comparison of the known R_f values for alanine will identify alanine for each solvent. ✓

ⓔ This would be a typical quality of written communication question in A2 Unit 2. Make sure you name two different solvents — one organic solvent and one solvent that is a mixture of ethanol and a strong mineral acid usually provides a good separation of amino acids. The R_f values in a particular solvent will always be the same for an amino acid provided the same support (paper in this case) is used.

Question 3

A mixture of butan-2-ol and methanol is separated using gas–liquid chromatography (GLC). The chromatogram is shown below.

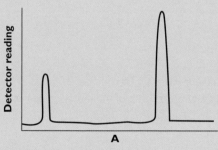

(a) What label should be placed at A on the chromatogram? (1 mark)

(b) Explain how the chromatogram can be used to determine the relative amounts of each component of the mixture. (1 mark)

(a) Retention time ✓
(b) The areas under the peaks give the relative concentrations of each
component in the mixture. ✓

ⓔ In GLC each peak usually corresponds to one particular component of the mixture but remember that some components may have the same retention time, so GLC alone is not enough to positively identify the number of components in the mixture. Connecting GLC with mass spectrometry would help to identify pure substances in the mixture by comparison with a database of known substances. A pure substance will have the same retention time under the same conditions of GLC.

Transition metals and electrode potentials

Question 1

Which one of the following is the electronic configuration for the titanium ion, Ti^{2+}, in the ground state?

A $1s^2, 2s^2, 2p^6, 3s^2, 3p^6, 4s^2$

B $1s^2, 2s^2, 2p^6, 3s^2, 3p^6, 3d^2$

C $1s^2, 2s^2, 2p^6, 3s^2, 3p^6, 3d^1, 4s^1$

D $1s^2, 2s^2, 2p^6, 3s^2, 3p^6, 3d^2, 4s^2$

Answer is B

ⓔ This question relies on the fact that transition metal atoms lose their $4s$ electrons first. This is a common question and the obvious distractor is A where the $3d$ electrons have been lost from the Ti atom. D cannot be correct because it is the electronic configuration of a Ti atom.

Question 2

The diagram below shows reactions of $[Ni(H_2O)_6]^{2+}(aq)$.

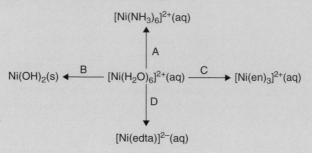

(a) State the colour of $[Ni(H_2O)_6]^{2+}(aq)$. (1 mark)

(b) State the coordination number of the complex $[Ni(en)_3]^{2+}$. (1 mark)

(c) What is the oxidation number of nickel in $[Ni(edta)]^{2-}$. (1 mark)

(d) Name a reagent that could be added to $[Ni(H_2O)_6]^{2+}(aq)$ to cause reaction **B**. (1 mark)

(e) State the shape of $[Ni(NH_3)_6]^{2+}$. (1 mark)

(a) green ✓
(b) 6 ✓
(c) +2 ✓
(d) sodium hydroxide solution/potassium hydroxide solution ✓
(e) octahedral ✓

ⓔ The oxidation numbers, coordination numbers and colours of the transition metal complexes are important for both the A2 Unit 2 examination and the A2 practical paper. The unknown inorganic compound in the A2 practical exam is usually a transition metal compound. You can almost identify it from its colour and then predict the reactions it will undergo based on your knowledge of transition metal chemistry.

Question 3

Using the standard electrode potentials below, choose the oxidising agent capable of oxidising vanadium from the +2 to the +4 oxidation state but not to the +5 oxidation state.

$E^{\ominus}/V$

$Cl_2(g) + 2e^-$	$\rightleftharpoons$	$2Cl^-(aq)$	$+1.36$
$I_2(aq) + 2e^-$	$\rightleftharpoons$	$2I^-(aq)$	$+0.54$
$SO_4^{2-}(aq) + 4H^+(aq) + 2e^-$	$\rightleftharpoons$	$2H_2O(l) + SO_2(g)$	$+0.17$
$VO_2^+(aq) + 2H^+(aq) + e^-$	$\rightleftharpoons$	$VO^{2+}(aq) + H_2O(l)$	$+1.00$
$VO^{2+}(aq) + 2H^+(aq) + e^-$	$\rightleftharpoons$	$V^{3+}(aq) + H_2O(l)$	$+0.32$
$V^{3+}(aq) + e^-$	$\rightleftharpoons$	$V^{2+}(aq)$	-0.26
$Cu^{2+}(aq) + 2e^-$	$\rightleftharpoons$	$Cu(s)$	$+0.34$

A chlorine

B copper

C iodine

D sulfate ions

Answer is C

e It is important to be able to recognise vanadium in its various oxidation states: VO_2^+ and VO_3^- represent vanadium in the +5 oxidation state; VO^{2+} represents vanadium in its +4 oxidation state; V^{3+} and V^{2+} evidently in the +3 and +2 oxidation states respectively. The electrode potentials are all stated as reduction reactions. The strongest oxidising agent will be found on the left-hand side of these half-equations. Iodine reduces to iodide, with a potential of +0.54 V.

$$V(II) \rightarrow V(III) \qquad +0.26\,V$$

$$V(III) \rightarrow V(IV) \qquad -0.32\,V$$

$$V(IV) \rightarrow V(V) \qquad -1.00\,V$$

The only reduction reaction that will make the emf of the first and second reaction positive is $I_2 \rightarrow 2I^-$ (+0.54 V). Chlorine would oxidise vanadium from +2 to +5. Sulfate would not oxidise vanadium(II) at all. Copper can only be oxidised, so it is not capable of causing an oxidation in another species.

Question 4

Chromium(III) chloride hexahydrate is a dark green solid that readily dissolves in water to form a complex, **A**. A few drops of sodium hydroxide solution are added to the chromium(III) chloride solution, resulting in a green-blue precipitate, **B**. Further sodium hydroxide solution results in a green solution, **C**. Addition of hydrogen peroxide changes the solution from green to yellow (chromate(VI) ions). Further addition of glacial ethanoic acid changes the solution from yellow to orange (dichromate(VI) ions).

(a) Write the formula for chromium(III) chloride hexahydrate. (1 mark)

(b) Identify the main species present for **A** to **C**. (3 marks)

(c) Write an equation for the reaction that converts chromate(VI) ions to dichromate(VI) ions. (2 marks)

(a) $CrCl_3.6H_2O$ ✓

(b) A is $[Cr(H_2O)_6]^{3+}$ ✓

B is $Cr(OH)_3$ ✓

C is $[Cr(OH)_6]^{3-}$ ✓

(c) $2CrO_4^{2-} + 2H^+ \rightarrow Cr_2O_7^{2-} + H_2O$ ✓✓

ⓔ It is important with any transition metal to remember the colours accurately because you may have to piece together a jigsaw of colours given even less information, for example in the practical exam. The colours of the individual transition metal compounds, solutions and complexes should be learned in case they need to be used for identification.

Organic chemistry

Question 1

Which one of the following is the mechanism by which bromine reacts with benzene?

A electrophilic addition   **C** nucleophilic addition

D nucleophilic substitution   **B** electrophilic substitution

---

Answer is B

ⓔ This type of question is common at A2 because all mechanisms have been met in AS and A2 and so it is expected that you will be able to choose a mechanism that matches the type of reaction. The π delocalised system in benzene is stable and rich in electrons, so the attacking species would be an electrophile and the stability means that benzene undergoes substitution rather than addition reactions.

Question 2

The reaction scheme below shows some reactions of organic compounds.

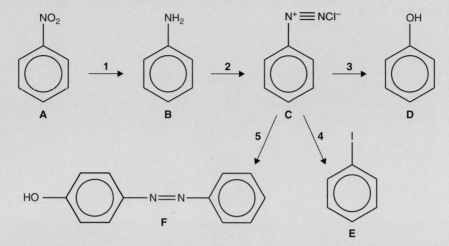

(a) The reactions are numbered 1 to 5.
   (i) Which reaction can be described as coupling? (1 mark)
   (ii) Which reaction is a reduction? (1 mark)

(b) What is the systematic name for E? (1 mark)

(c) What type of compound is F? (1 mark)

(d) State the reagents required for reaction 1. (1 mark)

(a) (i)   reaction 5 ✓
    (ii) reaction 1 ✓
(b) iodobenzene ✓
(c) azo dye ✓
(d) tin and concentrated hydrochloric acid ✓

e This type of reaction scheme is commonly used. You are expected to be able to follow through a series of reactions (some may be from AS). These reactions are very much A2, but reactions of functional groups cannot be learned in isolation. Try to link your learning together. You may be asked for the names of the substances, the type of reaction, the mechanism or the reagents and conditions required in the specific reaction. One of the most common reactions is reaction 2, in which nitrous acid (HNO_2) is used to form the diazonium ion.

Question 3

The organic compound below is an amide. Draw the structures of the organic compounds formed when it reacts as shown.

(4 marks)

The reaction scheme (top box) shows the central amide:

H—C—C—C—C(=O)NH₂ with substituents H, CH₃, H on the chain carbons and H, OH, H below, reacting:
- upward with NaOH(aq)
- left with P₄O₁₀ distil
- right with LiAlH₄
- downward with PCl₅

The answer scheme (bottom box) shows the products:

NaOH(aq) (upward) gives the carboxylate:
H—C—C—C—C(=O)O⁻Na⁺ with CH₃, OH substituents ✓

P₄O₁₀ distil (left) gives the nitrile:
H—C—C—C—C≡N with CH₃, OH substituents ✓

Central amide:
H—C—C—C—C(=O)NH₂ with CH₃, OH substituents

LiAlH₄ (right) gives the amine:
H—C—C—C—C—NH₂ with CH₃, OH, H substituents ✓

PCl₅ (downward) gives:
H—C—C—C—C(=O)NH₂ with CH₃, Cl substituents ✓

ⓔ It is important to be able to draw the structures of an organic molecule based on the reaction of a particular functional group. If excess reagent is used, this usually indicates that all groups that could react with this reactant will react.

Question 4

Proteins and polypeptides are made from amino acids.

(a) Write a structural formula for the formation of the dipeptide formed when two glycine molecules react together, and circle the peptide group. (3 marks)

(b) State the name of the type of reaction when amino acids react to form peptides. (1 mark)

(c) Name one feature of the secondary structure of a protein. (1 mark)

(d) Describe the tertiary structure of a protein. (1 mark)

(a)

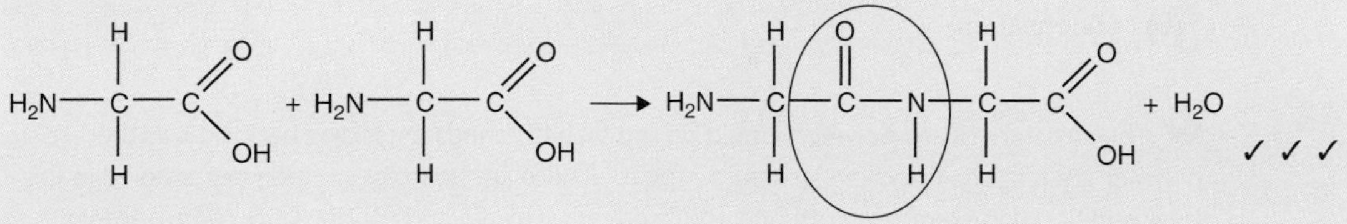

ⓔ The 3 marks in this question relate to the correct structure of the glycine, the correct dipeptide and the correct circling of the peptide group. This type of question could be applied to any given amino acid, but the process is the same and the peptide group is the CONH group. Don't forget the water as a product!

(b) condensation ✓

ⓔ Any reaction that produces water, such as the formation of an ester or a peptide, is called a condensation reaction. An elimination reaction is one that releases a small molecule such as HCl. Condensation reactions are a subset of elimination reactions because they produce a small molecule called water.

(c) alpha/α helix or beta/β (pleated) sheet ✓

ⓔ These are the main features of the secondary structure of a protein. These structures are held together by the hydrogen bonds between the C=O and N−H in the protein chain.

(d) disulfide bridges/ionic interactions/hydrophilic or hydrophobic interactions ✓

ⓔ There are many features of the tertiary structure of a protein that relate to its final folding. Disulfide bridges are formed between amino acid residues containing sulfur. Some side chains of amino acids are hydrophobic and some hydrophilic. Charges between side chains also cause attractions.

Question 5

(a) Draw the structure of the repeating unit in polyethylene terephthalate (PET). (2 marks)

(b) State the name of this type of polymer. (1 mark)

(a)

(b) condensation ✓

ℯ The structure of any polymer should be shown with bonds extending each side, as the polymer is a long chain and the structure repeats. There are two types of polymer studied at this level: addition (for example, polythene, PVC and polystyrene) and condensation (for example, PET and nylon). You must understand that addition polymers are formed from addition reactions of C=C (alkenes) whereas condensation polymers are formed from condensation reactions. Condensation polymers can be hydrolysed in the environment as they are broken down by the action of microbes.

Knowledge check answers

1 base peak
2 H atoms that appear at the same chemical shift on an nmr spectrum
3 tetramethylsilane; used as a standard in nmr
4 red to blue
5 $KIO_3 + 5KI + 3H_2SO_4 \rightarrow 3I_2 + 3H_2O + 3K_2SO_4$
6 blue-black to colourless
7 colourless to pink
8 retardation factor $R_f = \dfrac{\text{distance moved by spot}}{\text{distance moved by solvent}}$
9 Iron is a solid; N_2, H_2 and NH_3 are gases. A heterogeneous catalyst is one that is in a different state from the reactants (and products).
10 $1s^2, 2s^2, 2p^6, 3s^2, 3p^6, 3d^6$
11 green
12 anti-cancer drug
13 yellow, blue, green, violet
14 1 atm H_2, 1 mol dm^{-3} H^+, 298 K (25°C)
15 $HNO_3 + 2H_2SO_4 \rightarrow NO_2^+ + 2HSO_4^- + H_3O^+$
16 electrophilic substitution
17 ethylamine
18 $NaNO_2 + HCl \rightarrow HNO_2 + NaCl$
19 It does not have four different groups bonded to carbon atoms.
20 It is the sequence of amino acids bonded by peptide groups (bonds).
21 A polymer is a large molecule that consists of many repeating monomer units joined together.
22 PET (polyethylene terephthalate) or nylon

Page numbers in **bold** indicate definitions of key terms.